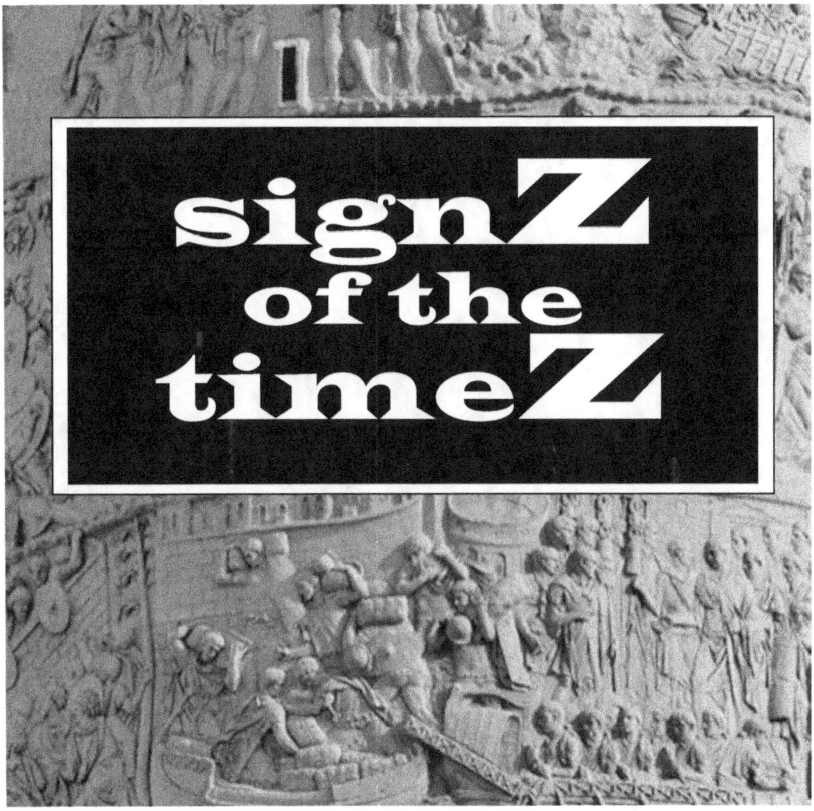

# signZ of the timeZ

by
# Richard Everett Londgren

Copyright 2018

# Foreword

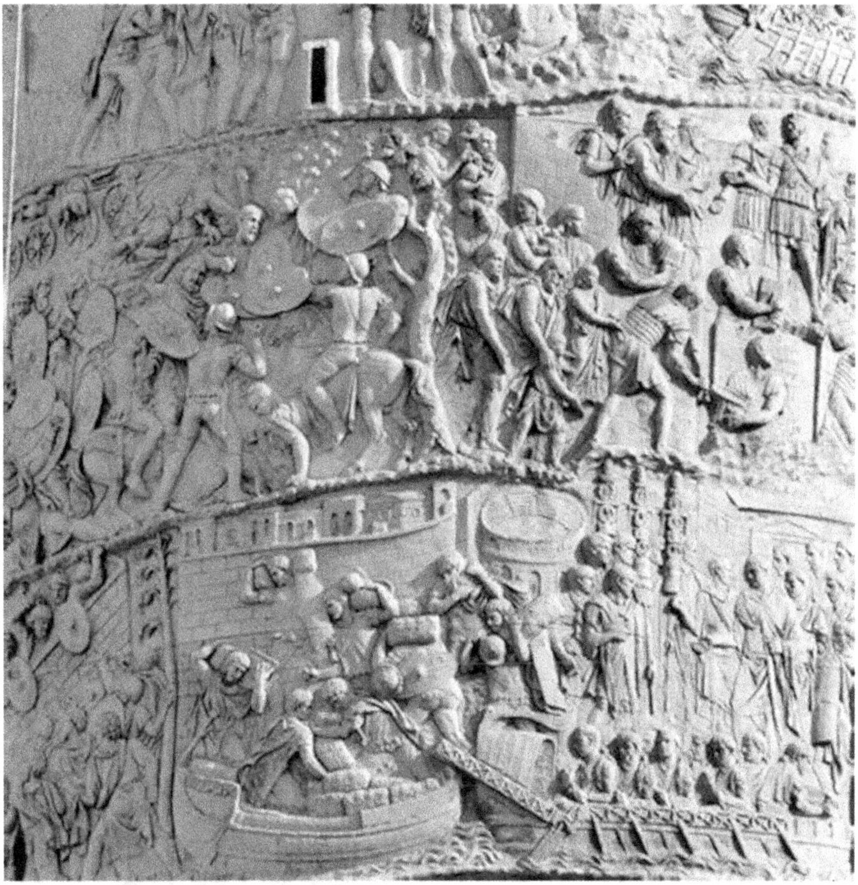

**Trajan's Column** in Rome makes a fitting cover design and theme for this book about signs now and in the past. To underscore the Roman standards for design of letters, I chose two typefaces that seem appropriate: **Wide Latin** for the title and subtitles and **Times New Roman** for the type of the text.

Created in 113 A.D., the column honors Emperor Trajan's victories. And the letter-forms in the column's base shown next set a lasting standard for typography.

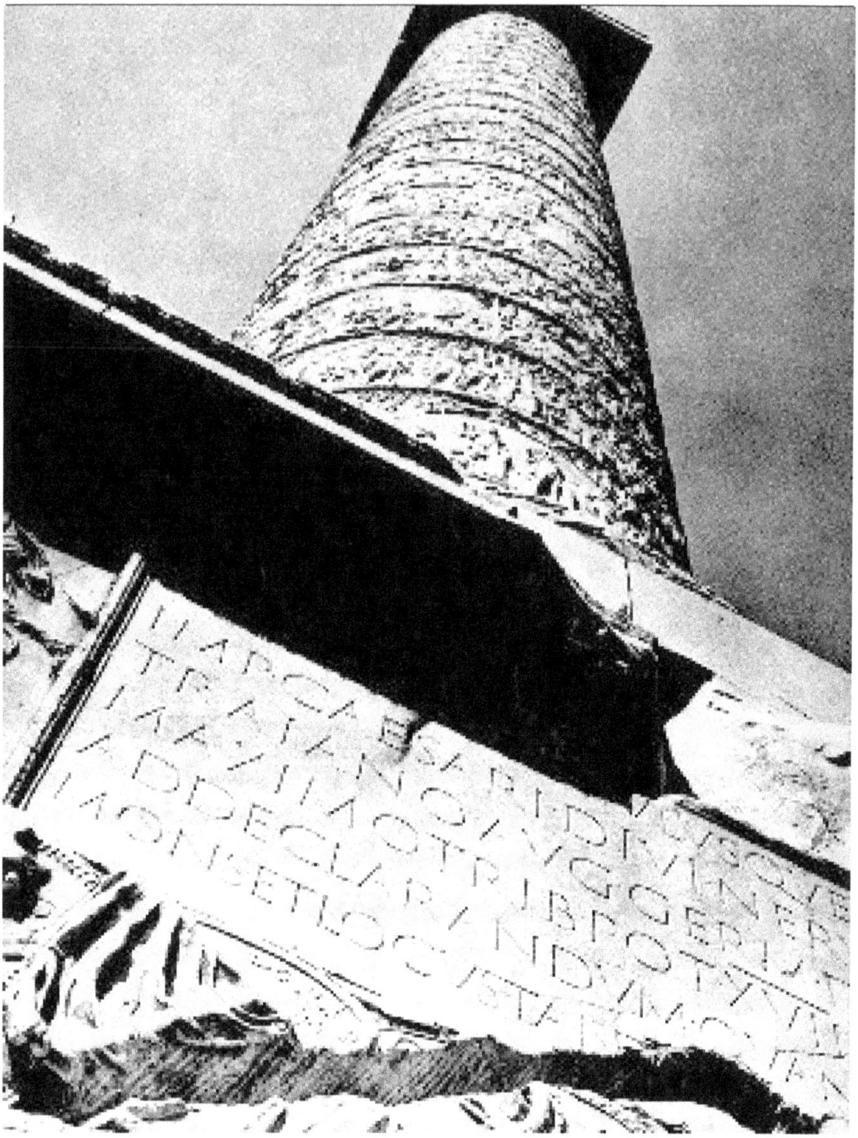

And carved scenes wind around the column like a comic strip—perhaps serving as a precursor to the current comic strips that depict dramatic victories when turned into blockbuster action movies featuring comic-strip heroes.

But don't assume from this link of the past to the present that I grew up in an atmosphere of learning about history and art.

Au contraire!

At age 5, I was enrolled in a one-room country school, as depicted in my story about our family's Country Store. But then I advanced when we moved to town…and to schools not much bigger (nine in my senior class in high school).

Though I was a good student, learning for me beyond the 3Rs came as "catch as catch can," as you'll see in following depiction of my interest in art.

Including my link to **signZ of the timeZ**.

# Richard Everett Londgren

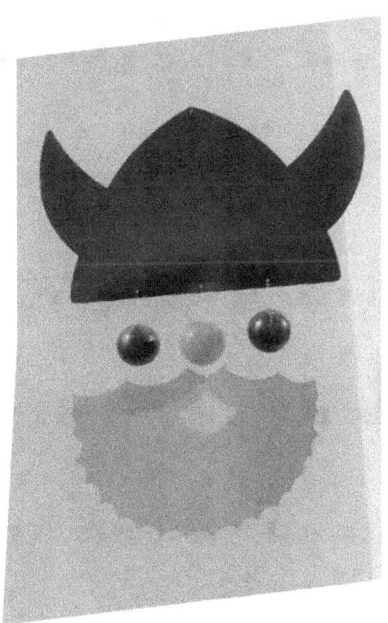

# Contents

**1**
**Commercial Art Call**

**2**
**From Rural to Reality**

**3**
**Gussied-Up Jeep**

**4**
**Go West Young Man**

**5**
**Calligraphy Appeal**

**6**
**Creating a Logo**

**7**
**Toolz of the Trade**

**8**
**Portland ▶ Tacoma**

**9**
**Corporate Career**

**10**
Employee Growth

**11**
Start the PresseZ !

**12**
▶Pacific Lutheran

**13**
SignZ at Home

**14**
Cal Lutheran Nordic

**15**
Church/Community SignZ

**16**
Promotion SignZ

**17**
Alphabet OptionZ

**18**
Readable Writing

**19**
Catalog of Books

I grasped the value of art at an early age, when my 3rd-grade paper- cutting of the Billy Goat Gruff and Troll won first prize at the Lyon County Fair in Minnesota.

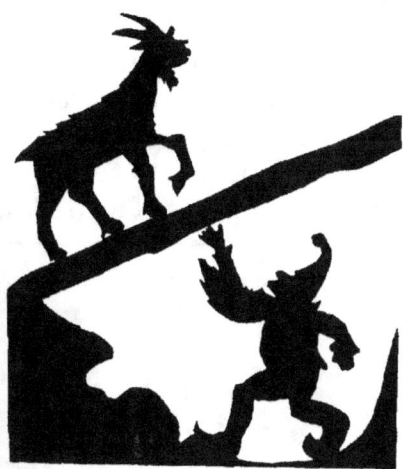

Thus, at age 7, I "invested" the 50-cent-prize payoff in "entertainment" via a season ticket to all events during the school year, including the "high profile" football and basketball games of the high school.

That early success in art encouraged me to create more cutouts, as I began zoo cuttings from the cardboard backs of tablets.

The other kids in my class caught on to my art interest, so their expired tablets didn't go to waste. A classmate collected the decorative front covers, but I wanted the backs to create my own decorative designs.

Then, I did get further attention, when our mother invited the teacher to take in a showing of my zoo creatures in our home.

Alas, no blue ribbon—or money—from that venture.

Many years later, I experienced a comeuppance during a visit to Denmark, when I saw the detailed cuttings by Hans Christian Andersen. One of his several talents besides his famous stories.

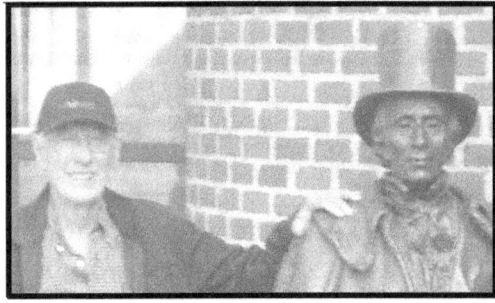

There I was, in Denmark, chatting with Hans Christian Andersen.

I learned that his writing proved to be more lucrative than his art cuttings. And he confirmed that the stories I favor, *The Ugly Duckling* and *The Emporer's New Clothes*, continue to be as relevant now in our era of the Internet as in his days of the 1800s.

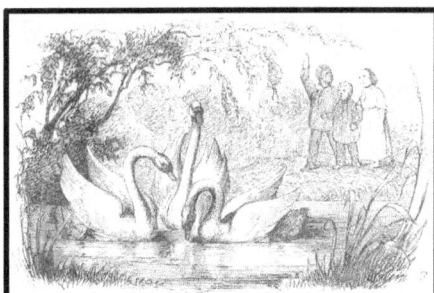
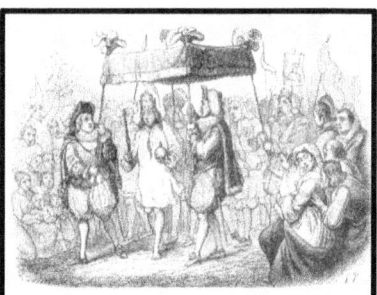

So I began to write and illustrate novels and other books. Including my book *Communication by Objectives* published by Prentice-Hall. Then two self-published books. Plus more and more.

Meanwhile, I kept my hand in writing, editing and photography for other organizations…with Lutheran communication included.

Teaching college classes led to more writing, and much more research about increasing the effectiveness of language and graphics.

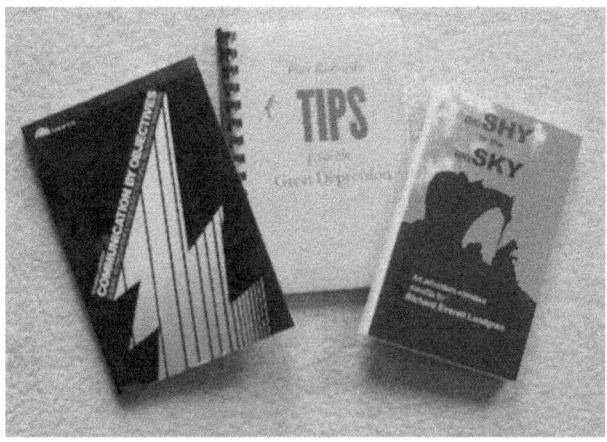

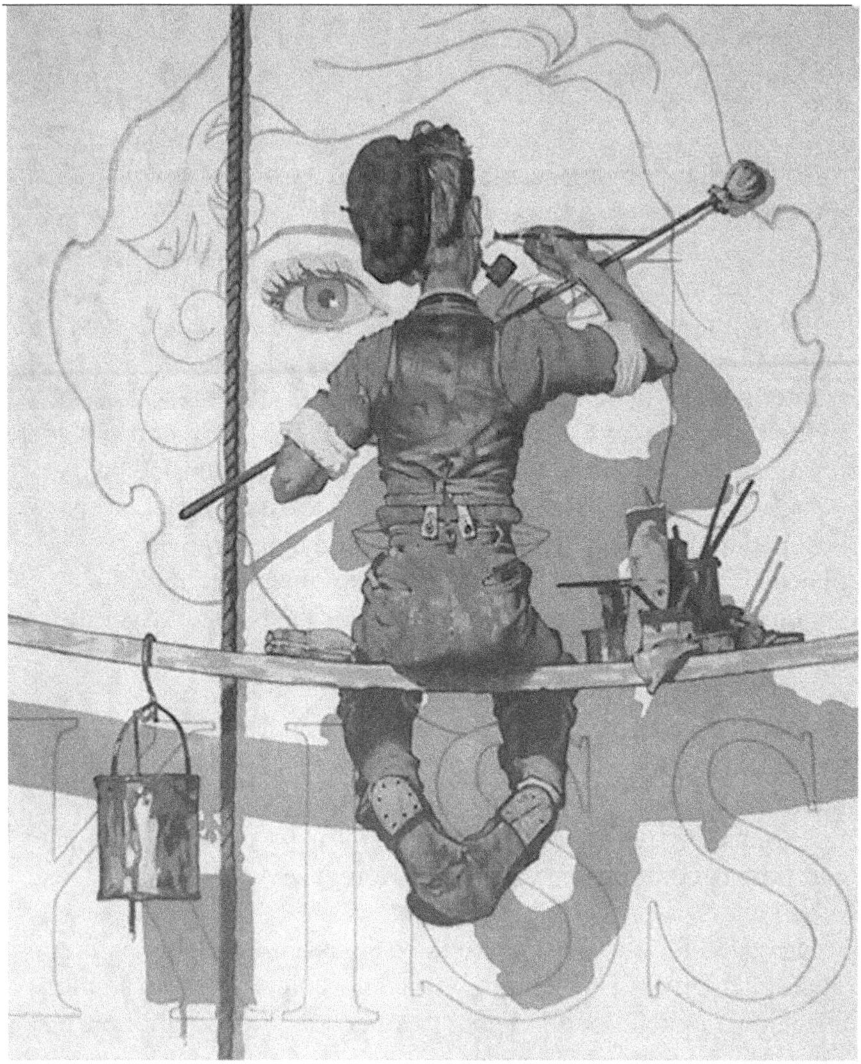

Previously, when I was about 10 and still a little guy… something up high…caught my eye.

A painter moved along on a scaffold (though not quite like the artist depicted here by **Norman Rockwell**), lettering a sign near the top of the tall lumber shed next to the hardware store in our Minnesota village.

In my mind's eye, I could visualize this "sky-high" occupation. Well, not quite like what we saw rarely when a plane towed a promotional sign through the sky. Or the dirigible signs I learned about much later.

Still, this sign-painting seemed intriguing to me—but imposing.

A little scary, to see the painter walking high up on a plank, with only a rope as a railing. But this painter seemed to be making a

**Graffiti timeZ?**
So, did such early examples of sign-painting encourage Graffiti? Well, Lynd inner-city kids did sometimes scribble with a crayon on a wall. And use chalk to outline for Hopscotch on a sidewalk!

living by practicing his "art." Maybe something for me to consider for the future. So, when the artist came down for a coffee break, I overcame my shyness in determination to learn more about his occupation. I learned about how he created a pattern with holes punched in the outline of the sign design. Then he pounded a "pounce" (like a small sack filled with carbon powder) over the holes to create guidelines on the wall of the shed.

The painter added that he liked to draw and paint other art for his own enjoyment…and sometime to sell. When he detected my interest, he encouraged me to consider the sign-painting trade…and not just on buildings, but on trucks as well. Even fancy and fiery decorations on cars and motorcycles.

As I headed for home, I pictured myself as a master sign painter in the future. Unless I suffered my usual nosebleed from up so high. Then, on a more hopeful vision, I wondered how I might create a fiery look on my rusty bicycle.

Though I never became an "aerial sign-painter" like that, I did create for a friend an eye-catching cut-out (of course!) of a giraffe to go atop his shop of craft items from Kenya.

So, keep your eye open later for Ginny the Giraffe along with many other signs I created for purpose and decoration.

And my interest in sign-painting did show up many years later—in the story persona of a high school senior called the "artful forger."

Among other creations, that "Renaissance Kid" painted a decorative sign on the front of the sawmill of the "company town" near Seattle.

Here's the gist of the story, as summarized by newspaper editor Scoop Johnson in the story:

> Too bad he joined the National Guard while he was still in high school, said a calmer Scoop. The University of Washington was eager to get him, for all sports. The football coach practically slathered when he came out to check on Neil. But Uncle Sam wanted him more, with Hitler stirring up Europe.
>
> Maybe that sign on our mill will become famous, laughed company forester Charlie Strom. I remember when he painted that. Splotching paint for a woods scene with his left, adding another color with his right, back and forth. And later he painted the company name with his right. Turned it into our mural instead of just the name Skogland Lumber.

But the Army discovered the painter's talents too and eventually based him at Fort Hamilton in Brooklyn and enrolled him at Cooper Union art school in Manhattan. The aim—train him to forge German documents as part of the Army Special Services.

Now, back to our life: When our dad started a gas station in our Minnesota village, an itinerant sign-painter for Coca Cola rolled into town to erect and paint a sign for "Bill's Place."

We three boys hovered around the sign-painter and plied him with questions while he erected the sign and then lettered the name.

Later, we remembered him for two reasons.

First, the sign-painter Les Kouba eventually became a noted wildlife artist, with his art in a variety of magazines and calendars.

Second, later our sign had to be removed…and we three athletes salvaged the sign posts he had placed so we could erect our outdoor basketball hoop in our small pasture (with the hoop arena "fenced in" to keep our cows out to avoid possible "dung shots").

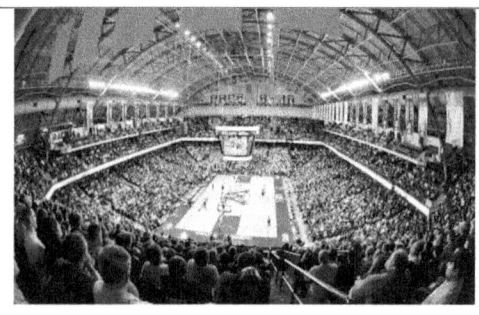

And that hoop stand led the way to remarkable results. Partly because of that practice area, we gained skills…enough that Duane, the oldest of our trio, eventually earned all-state honors for leading the team from our little town of Lynd (population 218), Minnesota to the state championship game—which alas the team lost after 29 straight earlier wins.  But by helping set an all-time record for attendance at a high school game—more than 16,500 for the championship game—the team achieved a rare honor—*TIME* magazine ran a few sentences about Lynd in its one page of sports (before *Sports Illustrated* existed).

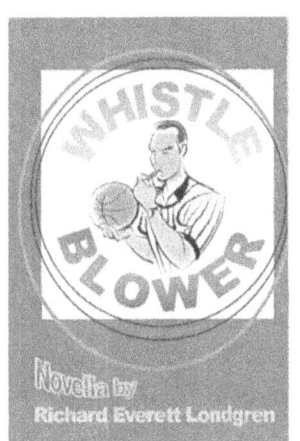

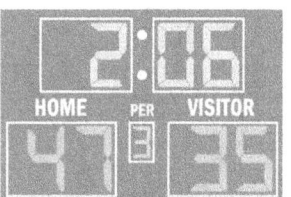

At that stage of Lynd life, by far the most conspicuous **signZ of the timeZ** would have been the lighted scoreboards that signaled the team's 29 wins en route toward the Minnesota state high school championship game.

But that ending was definitely not a score-board highlight. Instead, an inevitable disastrous defeat!

In my story *WHISTLE-BLOWER*, which grew partly out of my later challenge as a referee of high school basketball and football games, the scoreboard gets a starring role.

Well, not quite the scale of the University of Minnesota field house shown above, site of our Lynd championship game from my book *DAVID & Goliath* …or the significance of the Olympics

scoreboard shown later. But the scoreboard serves in **signZ of changeZ** as a milestone when college basketball began experimenting with the three-point shot and other ways to enliven a game that had become boring.

Ironically, the lights didn't flash the score at our Lynd home games, because the "scorekeeper" just reached through a window to hang on hooks simple metal plates with numbers…above one backboard to "score" the game. And sometimes the scorekeeper (usually a kid such as my younger brother Doug) got confused—and confounded the game by showing the wrong side winning. Then the official scorer had to send an urgent correction.

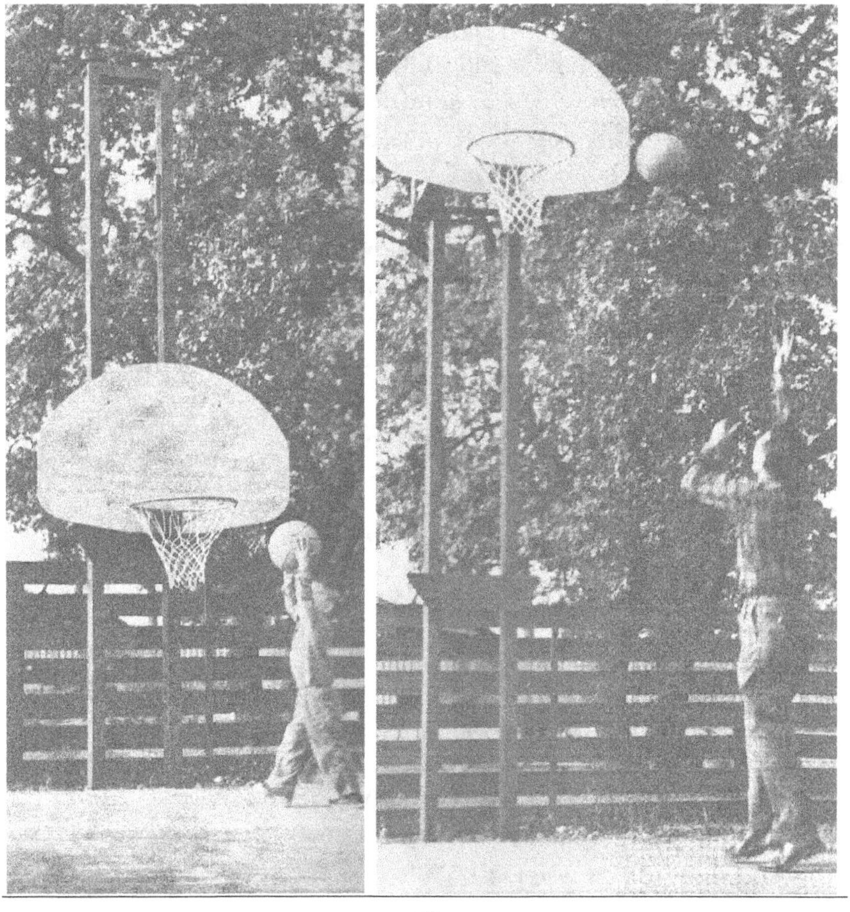

Now, let's segue back to the second phase of the "legacy of the posts" started by the Coca Cola sign from our family's store/gas

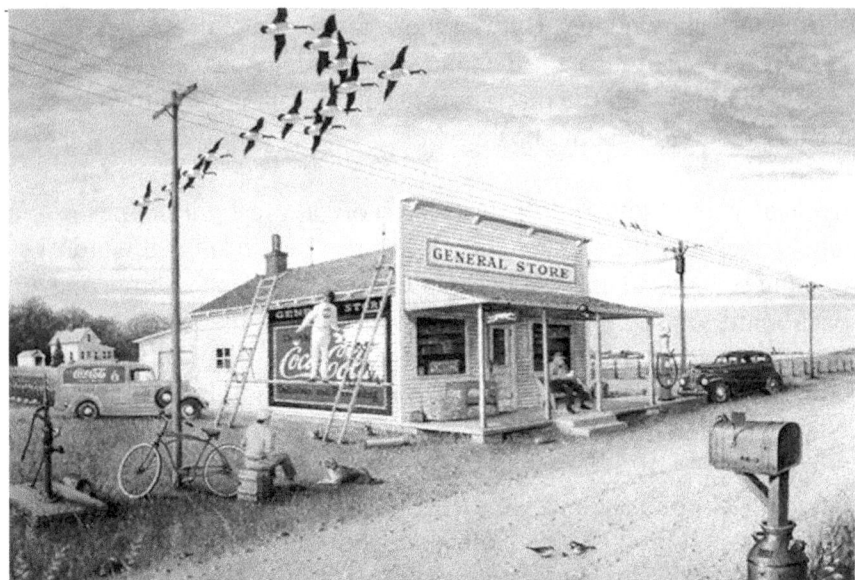

station. Years later, I created an adjustable-height basketball stand so both our young son Eric and I could shoot some hoops. Again, we salvaged recycled posts from an advertising billboard being removed. And that "hoop shoot" made news also—appearing this time in *Sunset* magazine and books (as shown below).

Now, to wind up this series of coincidences, the illustration (above) painted later by Les Kouba shows a sign-painter (perhaps based on his own experience) installing a sign on the building, not as a free-standing sign like ours—which we recycled into our free-standing basketball hoop.

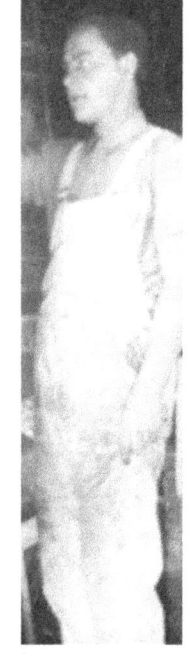

Well, I suppose we could have fastened a hoop on the side of our building. But it might have caused a lot of noise inside our house!

Les Kouba, shown at right from about the time he installed the Coca Cola sign at our gas station, later earned fame painting wildlife scenes.

His illustration of "ice harvesting" in Minnesota to get ice for "refrigeration" during the summer appeared in a Minneapolis newspaper. That scene

of sawing ice into blocks on the river reminded me of the ice harvested from our Redwood River, which we had to retrieve in the summer out of sawdust in a storage-shed at our local Lyndwood "amusement park." My brothers and I hauled those ice blocks to coolers when we worked during dances and special events at Lyndwood Park in our little town of Lynd.

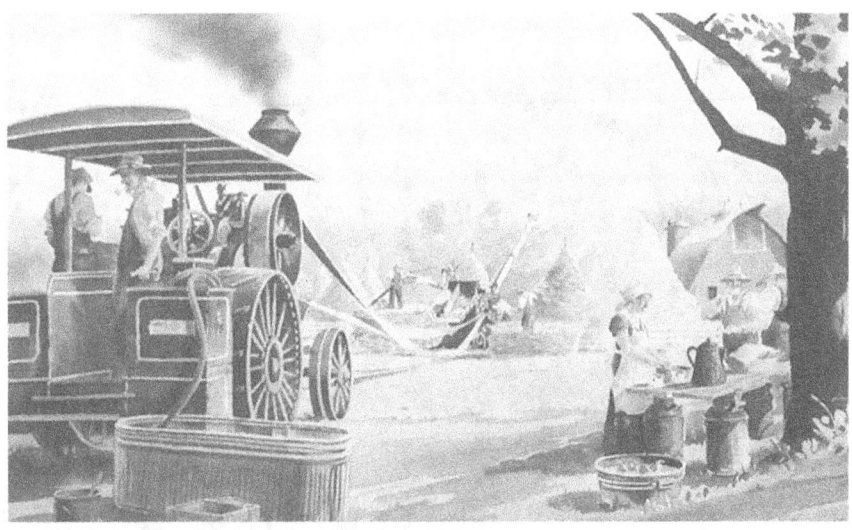

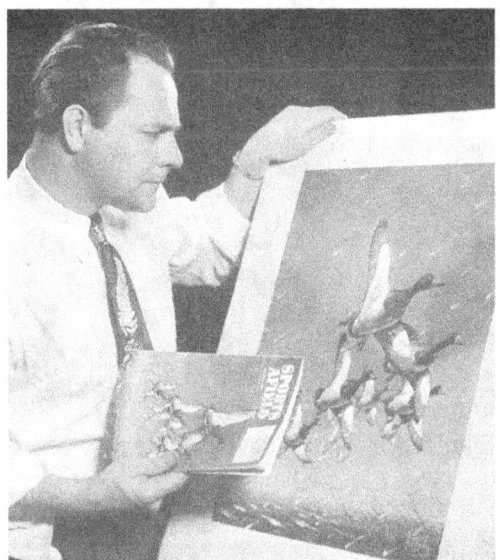

In winter, in contrast, Minnesota's blinding highway snow depicted in my own Krona Print (page 20) came annually.

And I won't forget the opposite we experienced in the misery of threshing grain shown in Les Kouba's painting above!

Les Kouba eventually earned national recognition for his illustrations, including this cover for **SPORTS AFIELD** magazine.

Like me with rural background and Art Instruction training (mine on another page), he served as inspiration for me to pursue in a career related to art.

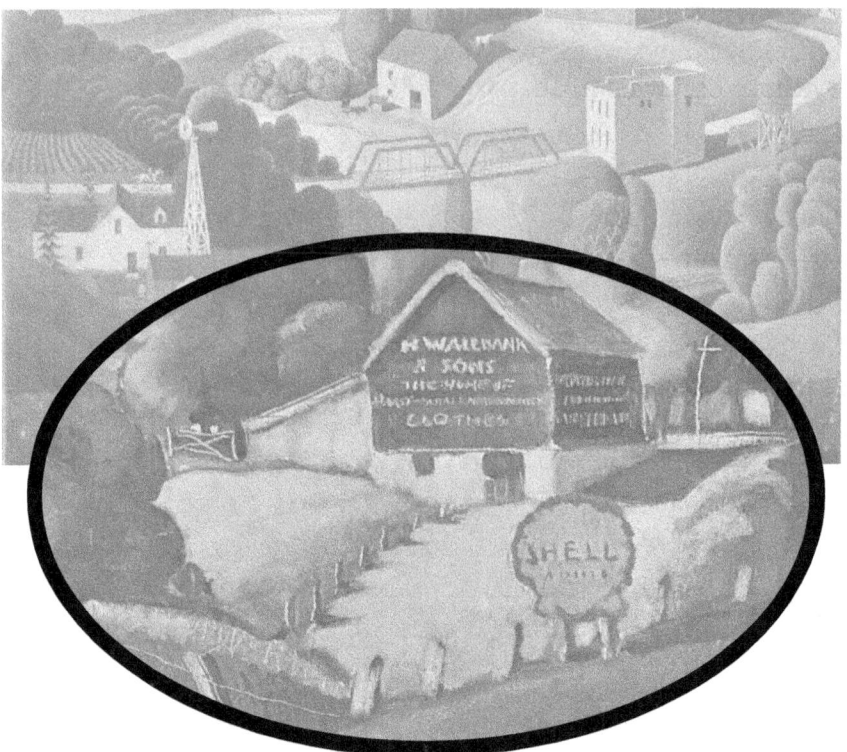

Another rural artist from the Great Depression, Regionalist painter **Grant Wood,** impressed me with his idyllic scenes from Iowa, such as his *Stone City* above. I combined that with an excerpt from another painting by him that depicts an advertisement on a barn and the Shell gas sign in the foreground. And that sign relates to my story about our **Country Store** in the '30s (next page), where the Shell sign declared that customers could get gas—and shop at our Country Store too.

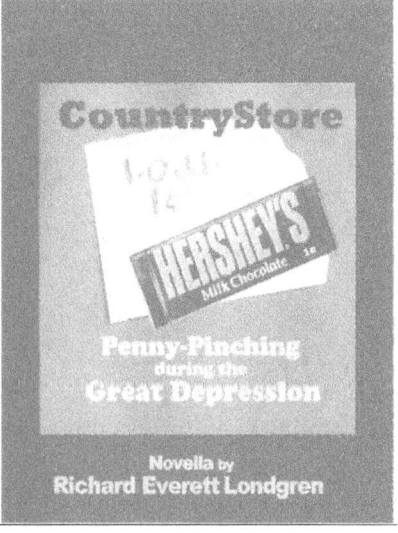

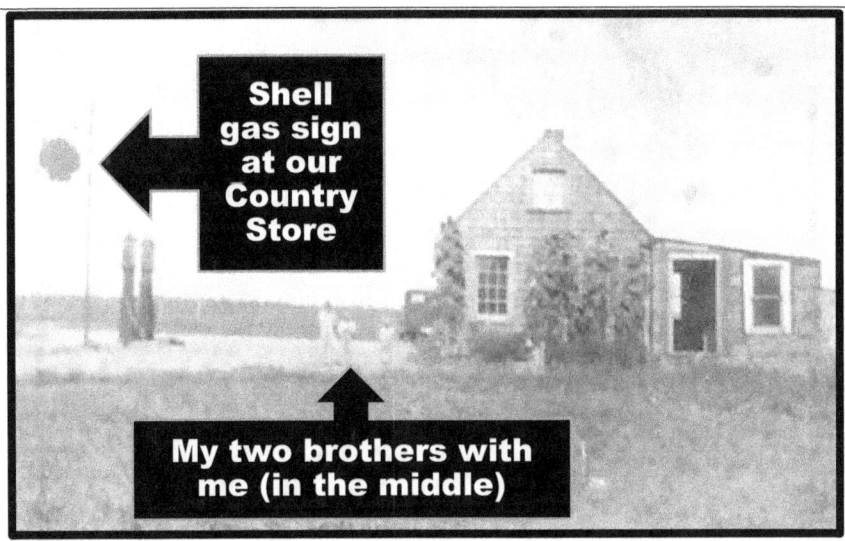

**Shell gas sign at our Country Store**

**My two brothers with me (in the middle)**

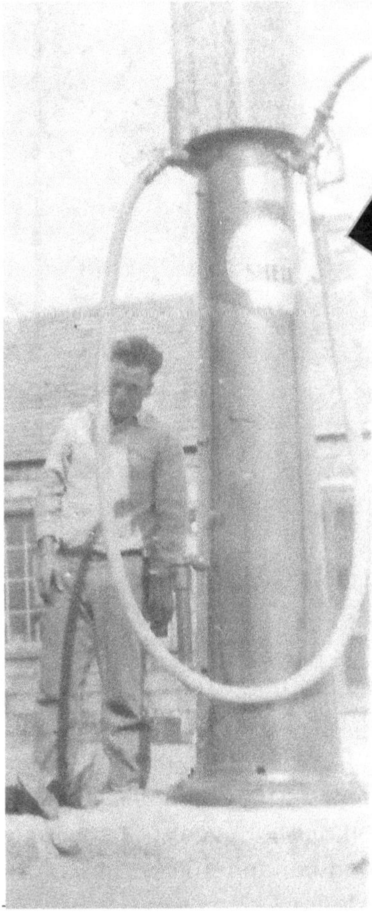

**Shell gas sign at our Country Store**

And here's our Dad, ready to serve a customer with the Shell gas.

And he no doubt invited the customer to consider our other wares…and to take time to have a cup of coffee.

Maybe catch the latest from the "soap opera" our Mother listened to on the radio. Unless the Golden Gophers football team from the University of Minnesota was on the air that Saturday.

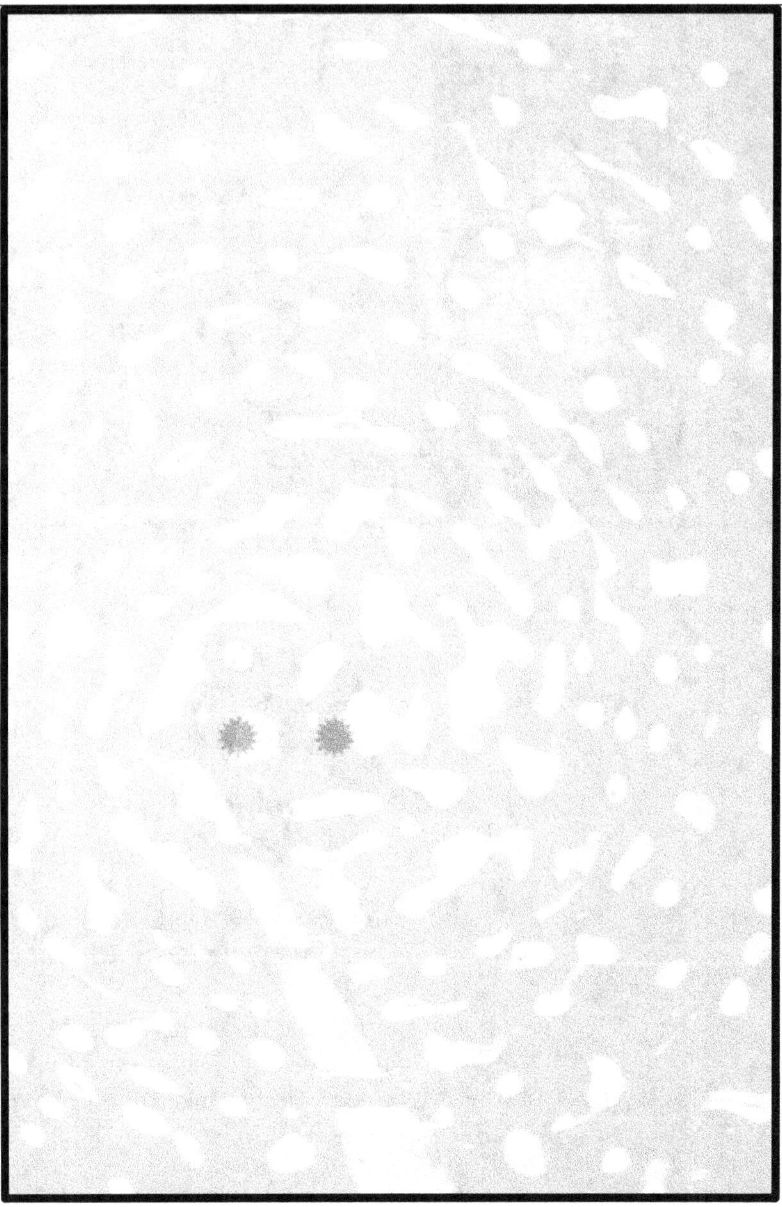

Picture this memory from Minnesota: In a sense, this Krona Print was "embossed," because I created the "snow" by dripping glue in a circular pattern on my "printing plate." When the glue dried, I printed with white ink on dark cardboard to reveal the "snow" pattern. In a second stage of printing on our antique press, I added the "tail-lights" in red, along with a number and title set in type: **"Snowstorm on Highway23."**

Another noted Minnesota-born artist, **LeRoy** (Runquist) **Neiman,** also painted for magazines, especially *Sports Illustrated* as with this painting of Larry Bird.

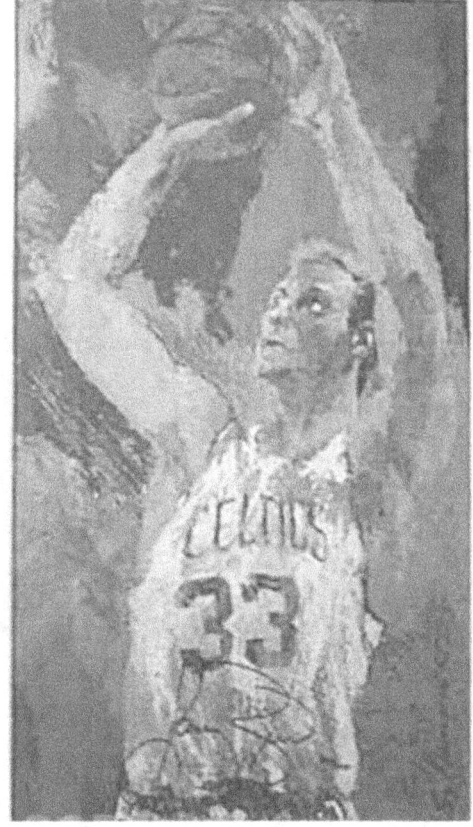

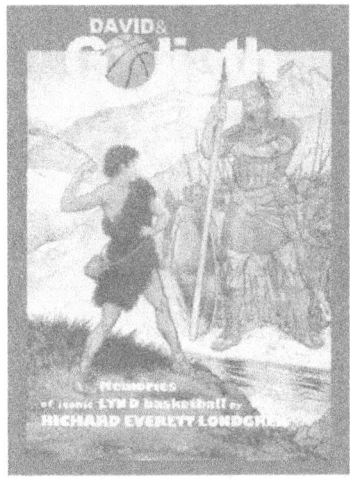

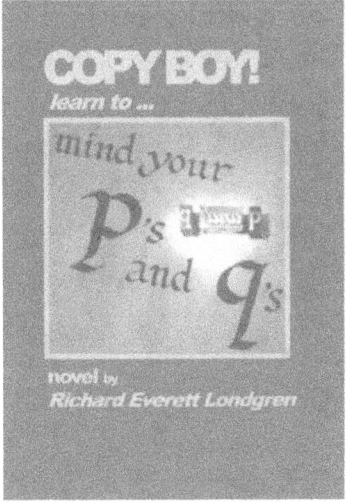

Like the players in my saga of our Lynd basketball team in *DAVID & Goliath*, Neiman was born in rural Minnesota, and Bird came from rural Indiana.

And my book *COPY BOY* takes place in St. Paul, where Neiman began his rise to success as a student at an art school in St. Paul.

But not a correspondence course!

Covers like these caught the attention of my brothers and me as we aspired in athletics. Our older brother Duane starred on the DAVID team from tiny Lynd. So I included a team like that in my novel *Whistle-Stop* in Lincoln, Minnesota (a town and school a bit like Lynd, with a hardware and lumber business too).

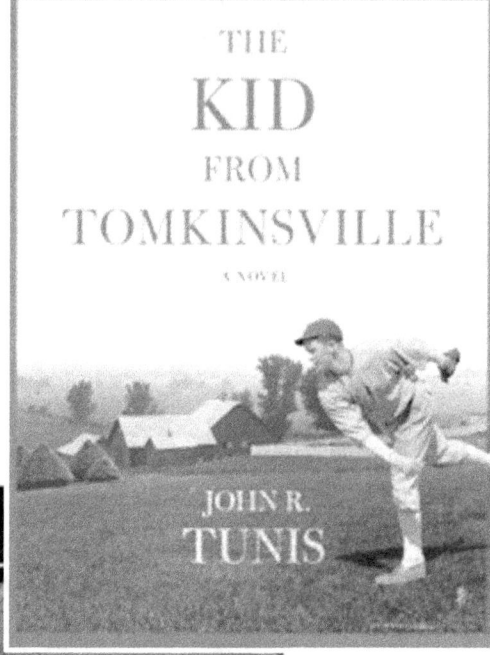

THE

KID

FROM

TOMKINSVILLE

A NOVEL

JOHN R.
TUNIS

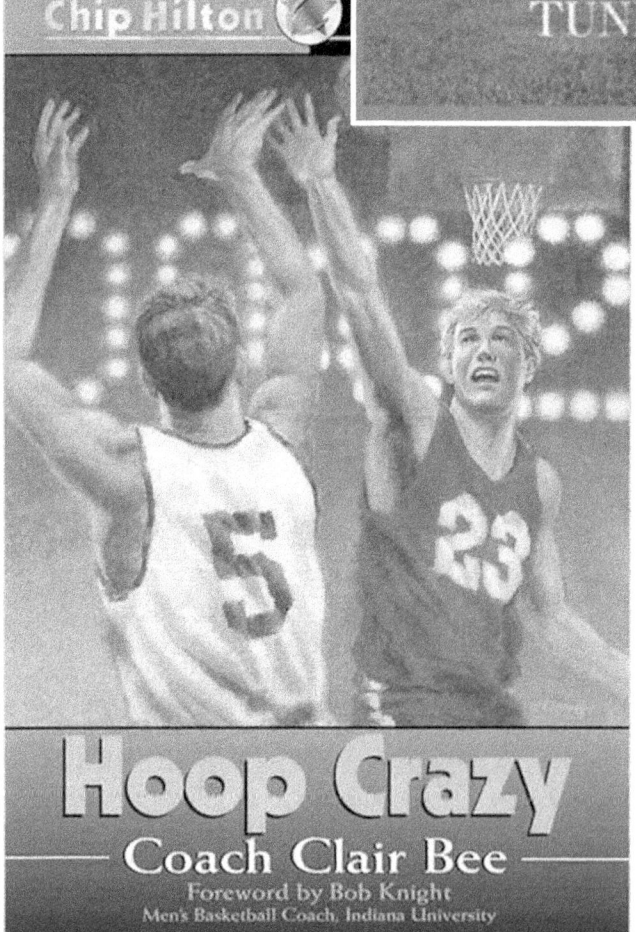

Chip Hilton

Hoop Crazy

Coach Clair Bee

Foreword by Bob Knight
Men's Basketball Coach, Indiana University

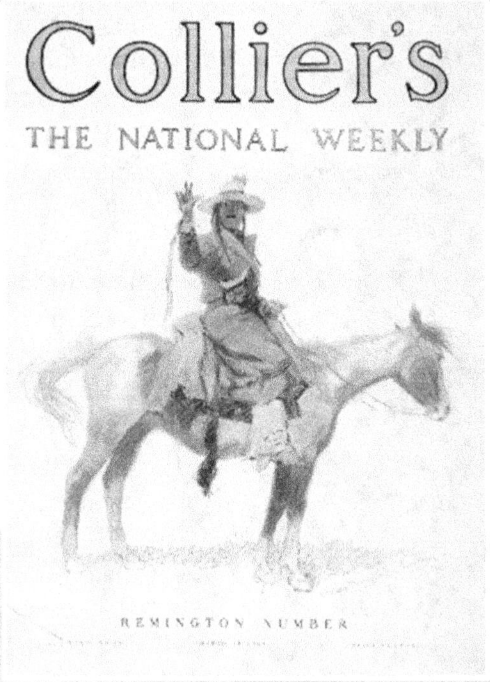

**Collier's**

THE NATIONAL WEEKLY

REMINGTON NUMBER

Incidentally, book and magazine covers and even the book spines can serve as effective **signz** to beckon potential readers.

Artist **Frederic Remington** (the cover of *Collier's* at left) and **Charles Russell** painted the West. So did Scandinavian-Americans **Olaf Carl Seltzer** and **Gunnar Widforss** (depictions of the Grand Canyon). **Carl Oscar Borg** painted as well as creating sets for movies. And, from high school, I remember great novels, such as *The Last of the Mohicans*, with illustrations by **N. C. Wyeth**.

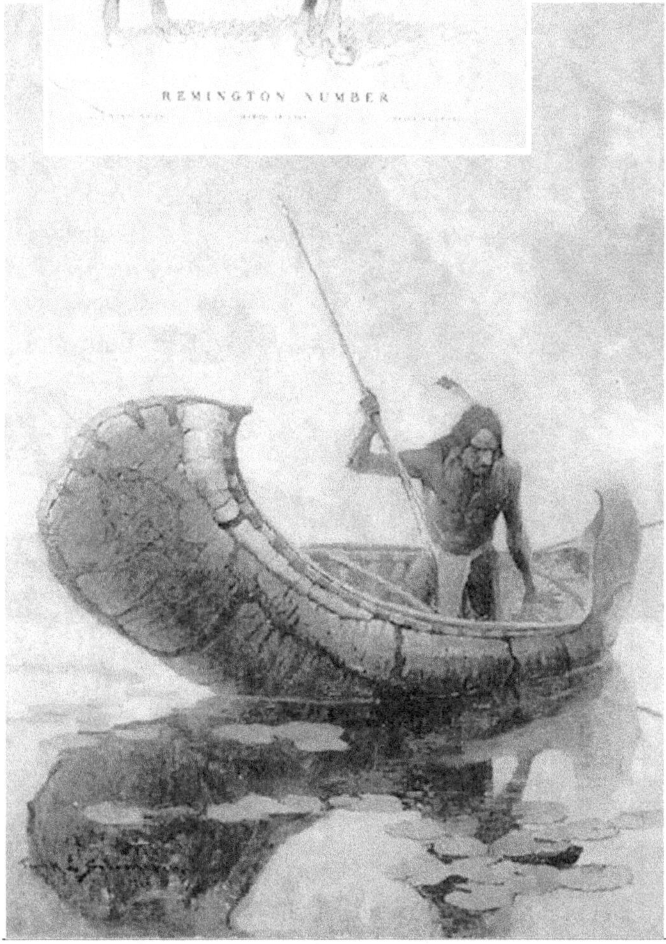

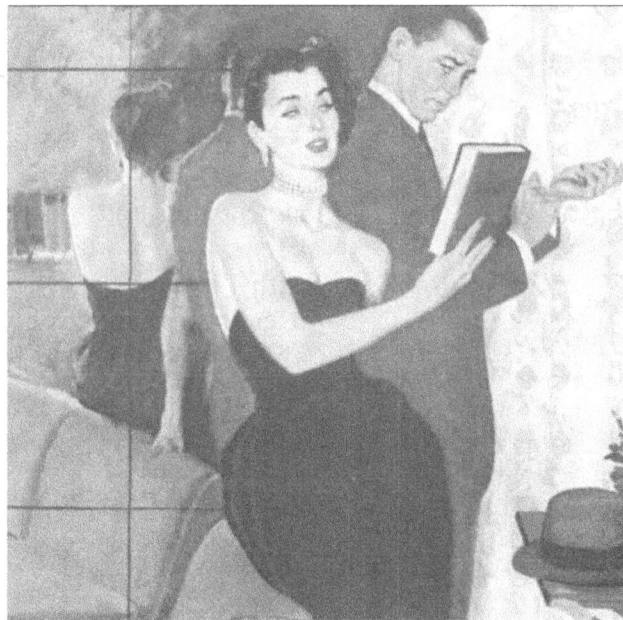

Meanwhile, illustrators helped "draw" readers to popular magazines in the heyday of short stories by noted authors.

And **Charles Dana Gibson** painted the "feminine ideal" with his **Gibson Girls.**

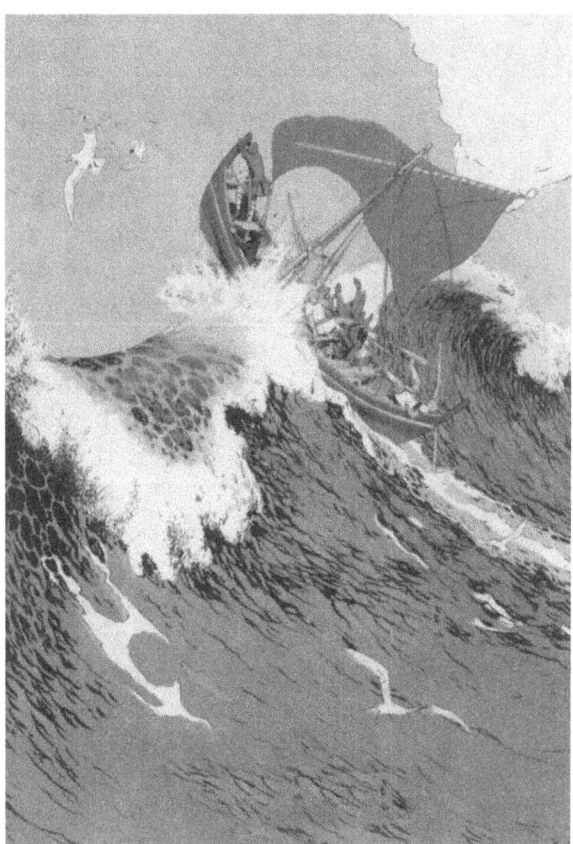

Newspapers included comic-strip art such as *Prince Valiant* (left) and *Steve Canyon* (below).

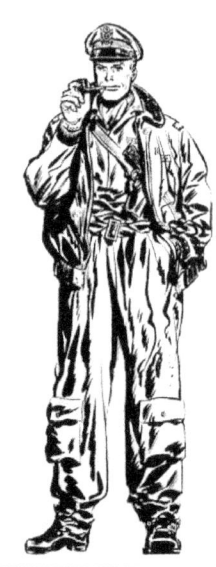

# Rural to Reality

Like Les Kouba, I grew up in rural Minnesota. He on a farm, me on a town-farm where we raised much of our own food with a garden for a variety of vegetables, lots of eggs, and milk from our cows (as already noted, fenced out to prevent "dung-shots" in our hoop arena).

Later we moved two miles from our village of Lynd to farm the land of our Grandfather Londgren.

After a traffic accident killed our dad, I "inherited" our farm-work when my two brothers were called into military service.

But to try to be ready to move on eventually, I enrolled in a correspondence

**Richard Londgren,** whose two advertising drawings are shown at the bottom of this page, is a young man with excellent talent. Good at rendering, lettering, accessories, furniture. Would be a good man for department store or catalog art work. Twenty-two years old, unmarried. Will take profitable employment anywhere. Especially interested in employment in Portland, Oregon, or Los Angeles, California.

Address. Mr. Richard Londgren, Route 2, Marshall, Minnesota

*Below by Richard Londgren.*

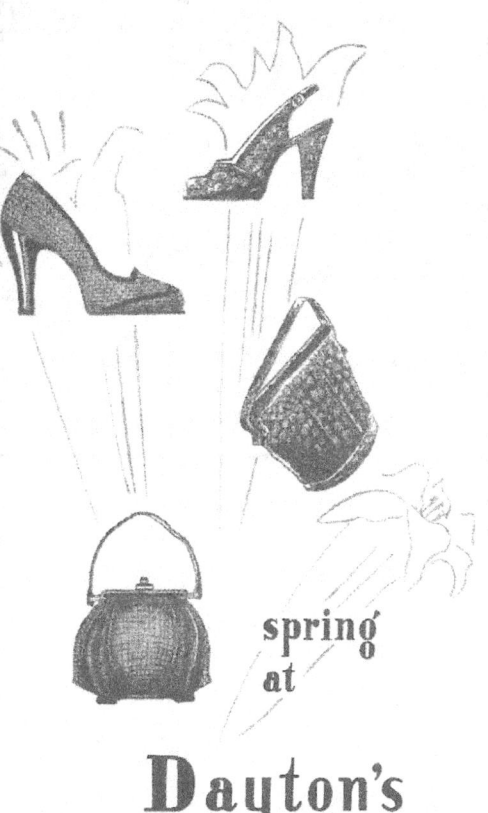

spring at

**Dayton's**

course called, appropriately, Art Instruction. Once again, encouraged by our mother as a way for me to break free and find my way in life. Again, coincidentally, Les Kouba had studied earlier via that school in Minneapolis.

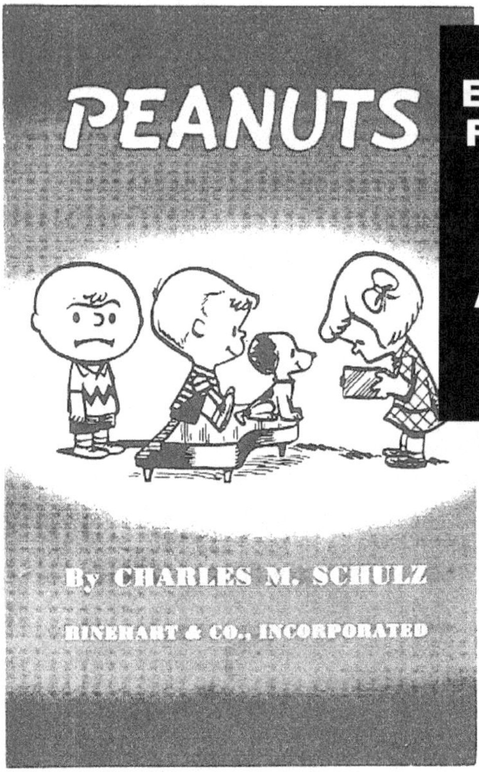

**PEANUTS**

**Excerpts from the Fall 1952 issue of**

**The Illustrator**

**Published by Art Instruction**

By CHARLES M. SCHULZ

RINEHART & CO., INCORPORATED

*Cover design of the cartoon book PEANUTS by Charles M. Schulz.*

And, after several months of study, I got the mention (previous page) in *The Illustrator* published by Art Instruction. Incidentally—or not so incidentally—the publication also announced the recent success of Art Instruction teacher and former student Charles Schulz.

For me, that bit of publicity—and luck—helped me land a job and get on-the-job training as a commercial artist when our mother and my two sisters and I moved to Mankato, Minnesota. Our mother then went back to college to complete her four-year degree, beyond the more-limiting degree she had earned long before.

P.S. Check the hope mentioned for me in box on the previous page—I had stated I'd like to live in Portland or Los Angeles.

Well, I finally made it to both places, ending up in Los Angeles now after a long pause along the way for college and a corporate career and church volunteerism in Tacoma, Washington. So luck—with maybe some talent and training mixed in—prevailed. But along the way, I connected with Charlie Brown another way—my kite refused to fly. As a kid, I spent a lot of time decorating the

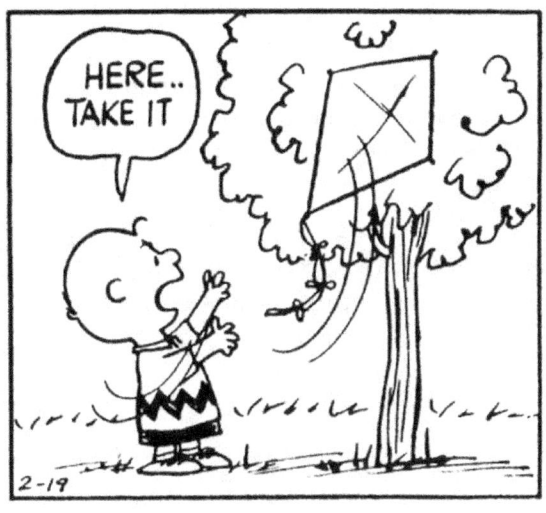

kite's thick kraft paper, but not on flight design of my kite. It proved to be too heavy to take off. Or just badly designed. Wright Brothers and **Ben Franklin**—where were you when I needed you?

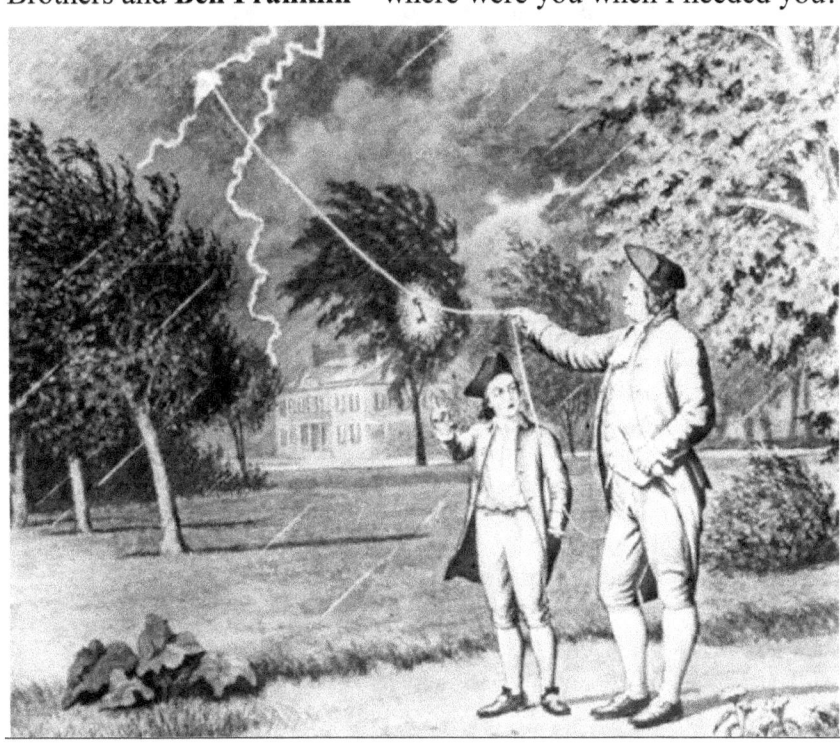

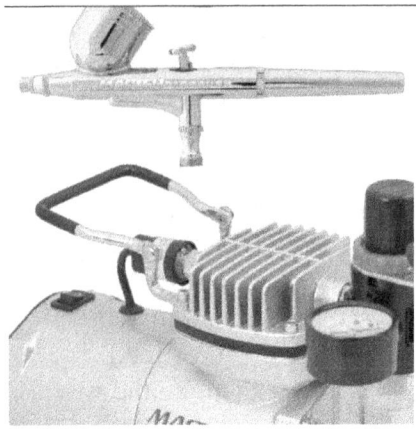

In Mankato, I learned photo retouching—masking, airbrushing, cleaning and repeating. Then, parts of equipment for a catalog emerged from the murky background of the machine.

Like an artist-friend who helps surgeons by retouching photos to sort internal body parts from blood and guts by airbrushing.

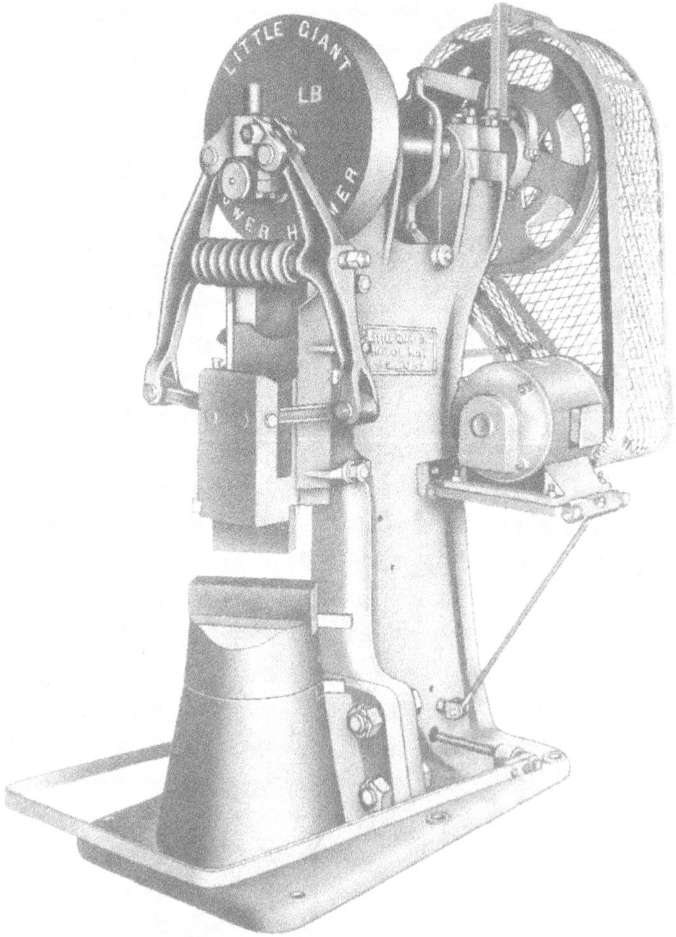

My position as an artist in Mankato included much on-the-job training, including the use of the artist's airbrush for creating and modifying advertisements and illustrations for catalogs.

Though an air brush also can be employed to add fiery designs to Hot Rods, I never got a shot at that.

But I did take evening classes in photography, and I studied regularly at the nearby public library. Part of my life-long learning.

At one time, like so many other hopeful artists, I had wished to land an opportunity as an animator at Disney.

If I had stuck around an earlier time while visiting Aunt Evelyn in Los Angeles, I might have had a shot at it. A long shot.

Finally, here I am at a Disney display in the Reagan Library just a few miles from where we live now. Well, as shown here, I had my brief photo-op fling as an animator.

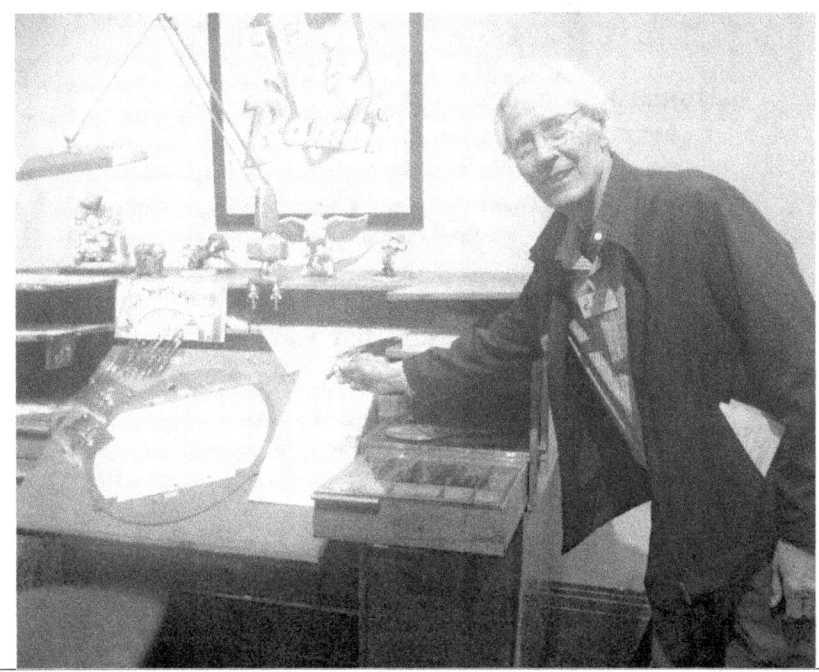

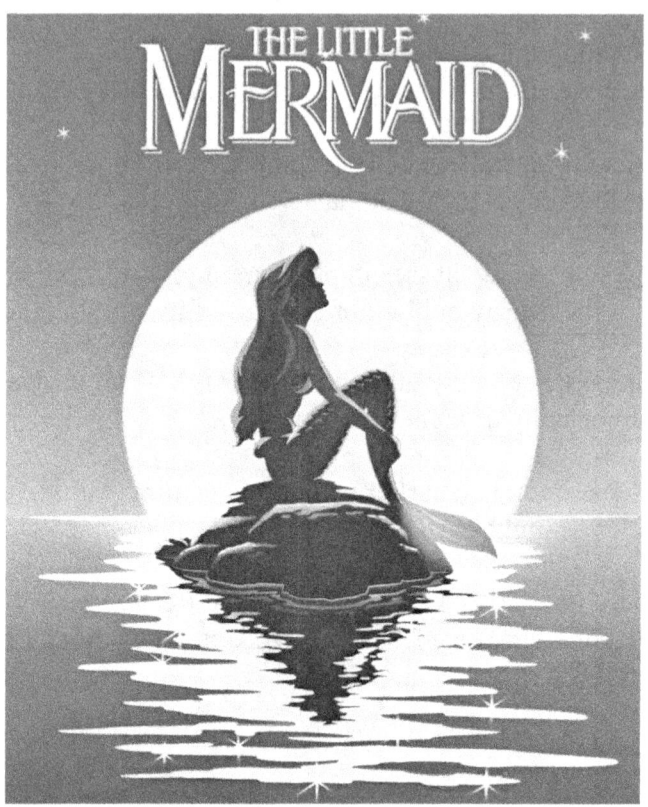

Ironically, our next-door neighbor in Tacoma was related to an animator. His cousin's Disney projects included illustrating *The Little Mermaid*, the story by Hans Chistian Andersen of Denmark.

Appropriately, our neighbor's name was "Anderson," and his relative was "Berg." Both Norwegian-Americans, not Danish.

# Gussied-Up Jeep

With hope motivating me to study and practice, I turned my hand at a start of commercial art by creating a "logo" to apply to the doors of our four-wheel-drive Jeep. And to a letterhead and card.

We used that Jeep as a supplemental tractor as well as a road vehicle. To change it from al fresco, I first had to build a plywood cab—and then add such fringes as a heater, radio and spotlight. Before I installed the plywood doors, I decided our Jeep should also have an interesting design related to our

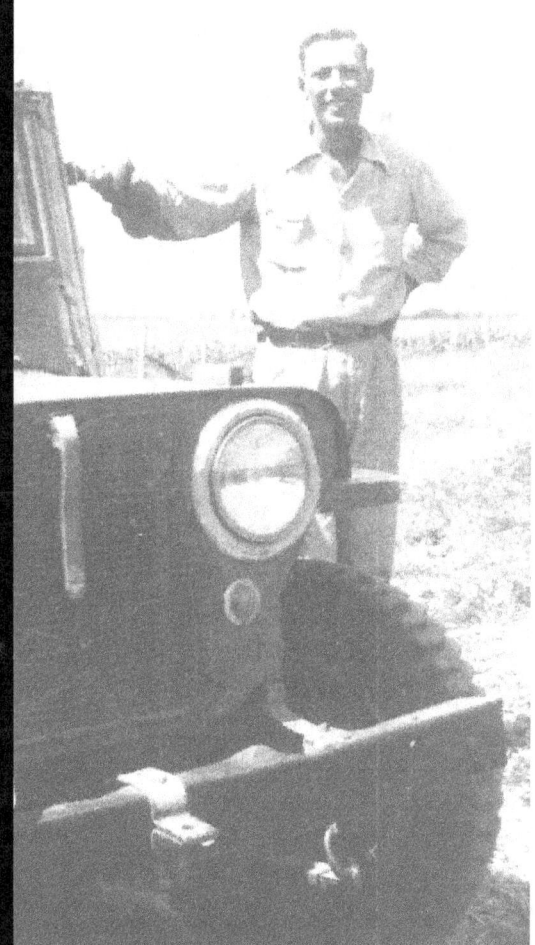

family. So, as a self-imposed assignment in art, I painted a bucking bronco and the name 3-L Ranch (for us three brothers).

Hardly appropriate in Minnesota—a bronco or a ranch. But we enjoyed the attention

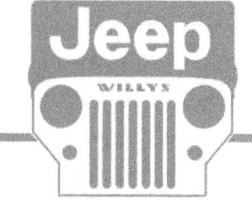

it created. Our Jeep featured the Willys name, and now some contemporary Jeep owners have added the Willys logo as an extra detail.

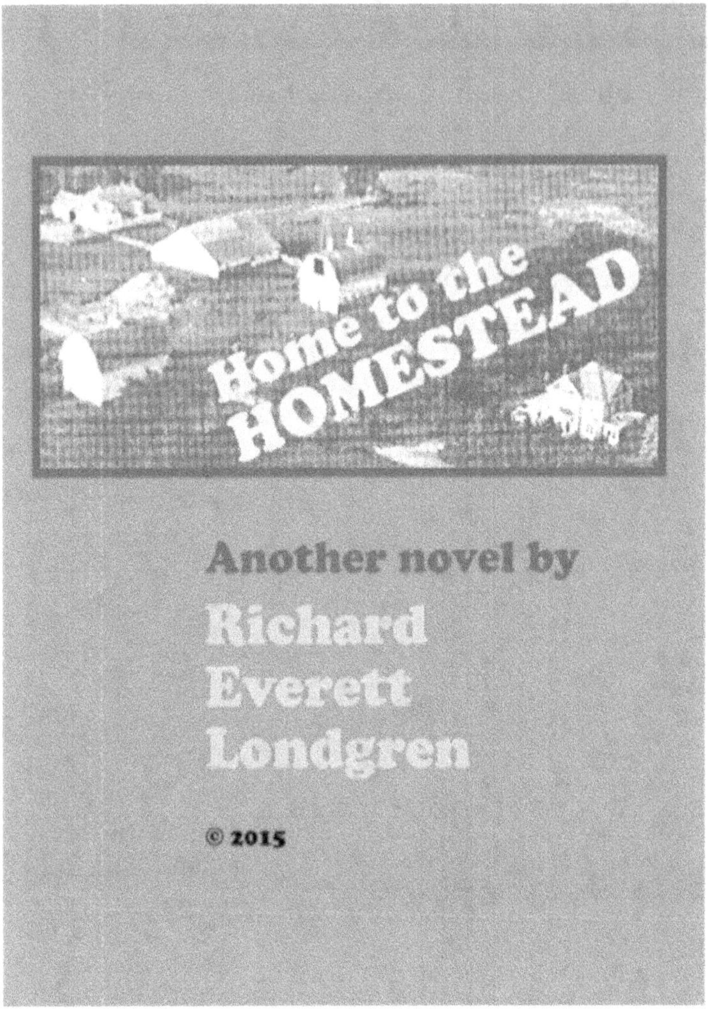

**Home to the HOMESTEAD**

**Another novel by**

**Richard Everett Londgren**

© 2015

Despite the sweat and strain of my short tenure of operating Grampa Londgren's farm, I did re-live that experience by using the aerial photo of Grampa's home-place on the cover of my novel shown above. I also incorporated some of his innovations in this story about a person of Danish descent (not Swedish like Grampa) re-developing the Iowa Homestead (associated with the U S Homestead Act) of his great-grandfather into a modern corporate headquarters.

# Go West, Young Man

*The Illustrator* a few pages ago reported that I hoped to head West. So, one cold Minnesota day our family of my mother and two sisters packed up and headed out on the Oregon Trail.

Not exactly in a covered wagon, but we packed (squeezed) what we needed into our Ford two-door club coupe.

Fortunately, no blizzards on the way, but we sure welcomed the mild moist weather and the green of Western Oregon.

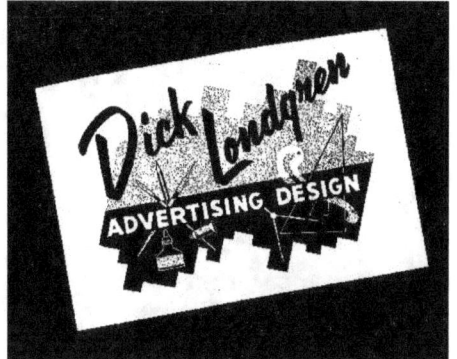

Then a job search began again for me. Armed with a new business card and art samples like shown below, I made the rounds.

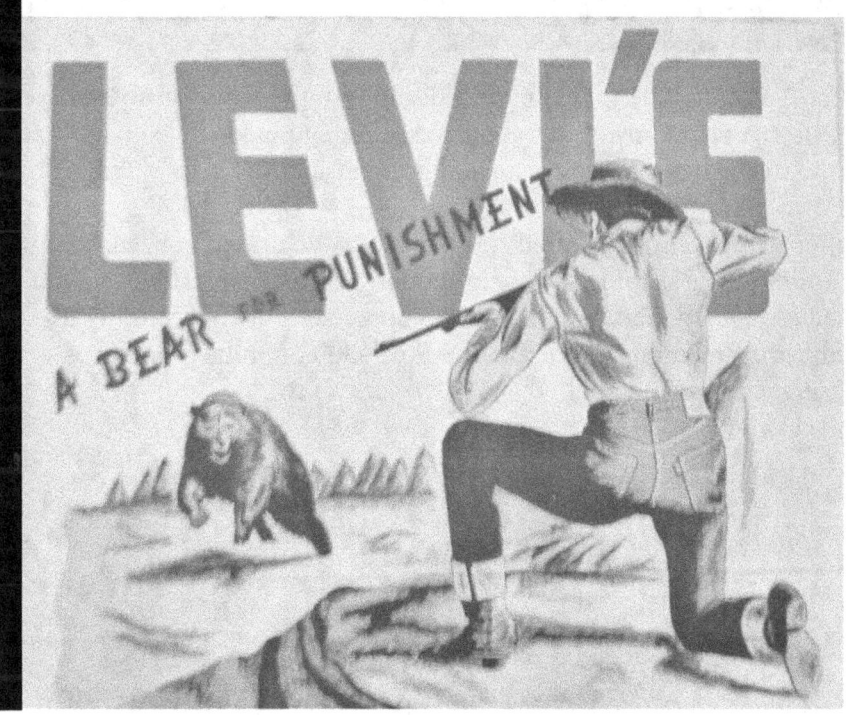

33

Eventually, I landed a position at a small industrial advertising agency. Low pay, low quality of work. But a foot in the door, and a chance to learn about the city and state and the media—and learn from others in the advertising business.

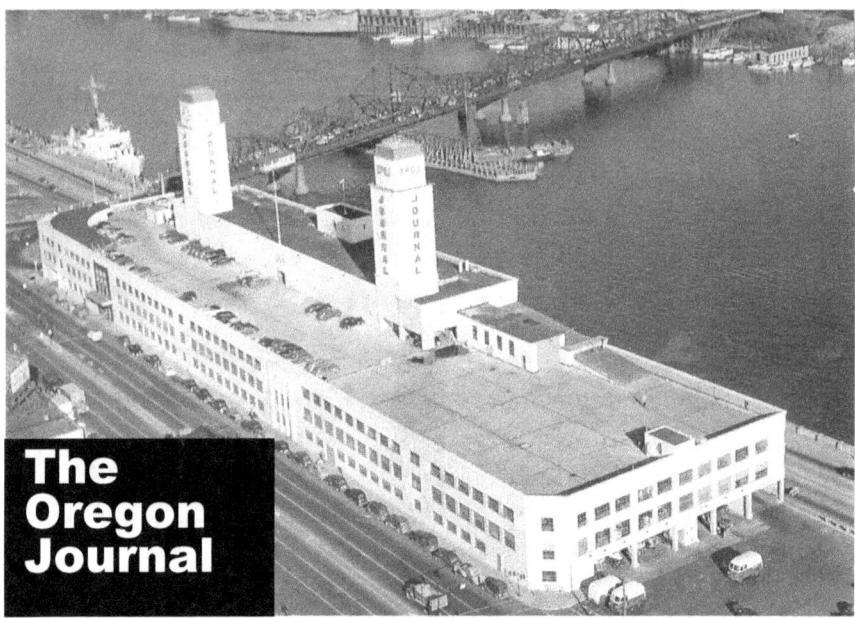

The Oregon Journal

That stint led me to an opportunity to join the art department of *The Oregon Journal*. As you can see, a big place—even parking on the roof. Huge presses inside. Biggest structure I'd ever worked in.

Fortunately, I had studied some perspective drawing, because my assignments including sketching many buildings for the advertising department. Again, I appreciated the opportunity to meet people and learn about the Portland community and area. Such as Mt. Hood below and the rivers above.

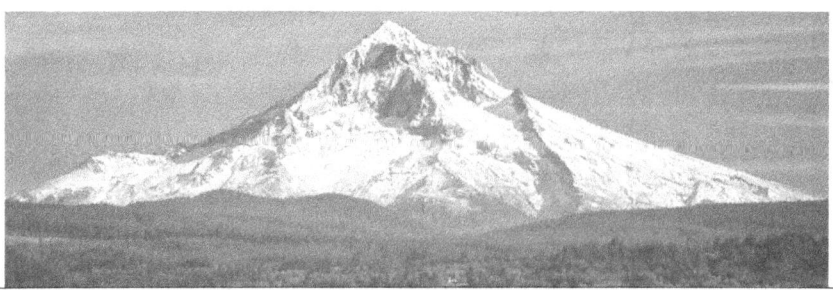

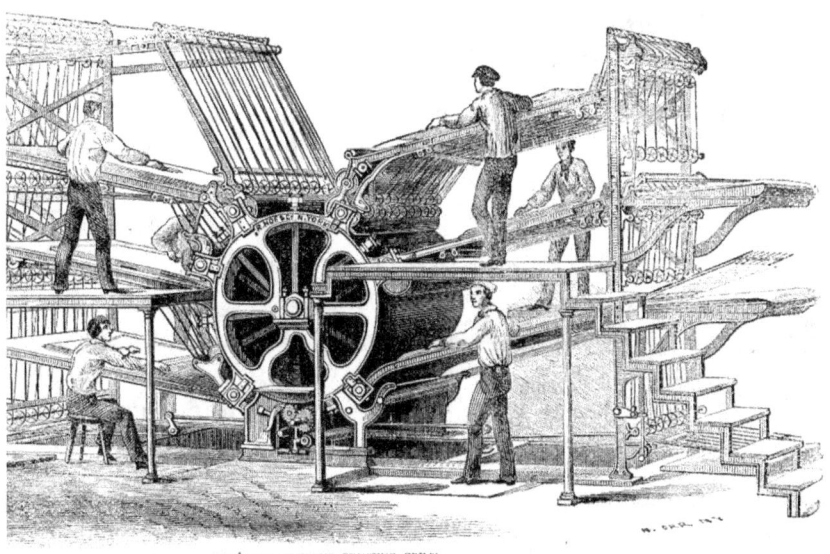

HOE'S SIX CYLINDER PRINTING PRESS.

I used to be assigned to take visitors, such as Scouts, classes or intrigued adults on tours of the printing operation in *The Journal*.

The giant rotary presses were much newer and bigger than this 1860 example, and impressive! The presses gobbled up the giant rolls of paper, with more rolls stacked nearby and ready for quick attaching to an expiring roll.

The curved heavy metal plates printed directly on the paper, unlike the later "offset" lithography process.

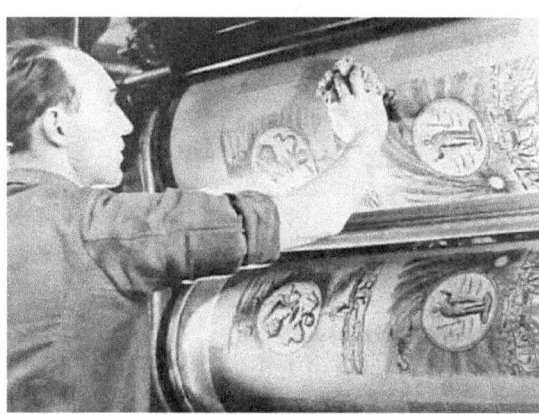

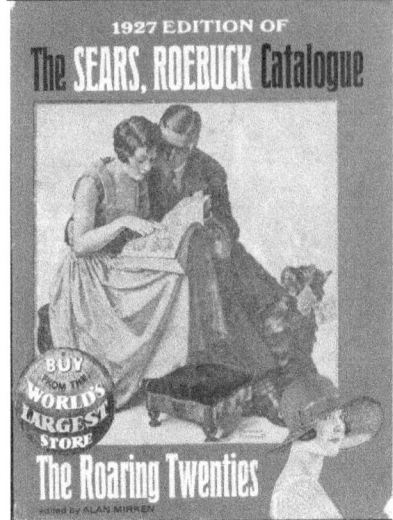

In a surprising but logical "throw-back" to my earlier life, the *Journal* art department kept a Sears catalog handy as a practical reference.

The mail-order catalog (Wards for us when I "shopped" as a kid) no doubt helped set the stage for the burgeoning Online business now. Small town merchants even fought the trend by rewarding kids to turn in their family catalog.

Though using the catalog as an aid to art surprised me, I certainly recalled its importance in "study" and shopping by our family. Later, even our kids and their friends turned often to the fun of our collection of the "big book" as well as the alluring Christmas catalogs in our "wish-book" library.

In my novel *Whistle-Stop,* I described the English teacher challenging her students to write concise catalog descriptions to work hand-in-hand with the illustration of the product.

Later, a public relations colleague told about his valuable experience in Chicago, writing summaries for the Sears catalog. Like another who credited the "education" he gained from writing classified ads for the newspaper.

In my book about *Poor Richard's TIPS from the Great Depression*, I reported about another stage of life for a catalog—in the "outhouse" where an expired catalog could provide entertaining "think and stink" perusal.

Then the "end-use" of the catalog occurred when pages served as practical toilet paper. At least when printed on coarse "pulp paper," not the less-usable slick paper of later catalog pages.

## SignZ of the timeZ!

# Calligraphy Appeal

My learning challenge continued in Portland as I sought to make up for my paucity of education in my Minnesota high school.

As I recounted earlier, basketball reigned as king in our tiny town and school. As our family emerged slowly from the Great Depression, my brothers and I encountered almost an economic stone wall about attending college. Then as I recovered from this educational vacuum, I met other young people of my age, and they shocked me with how much they knew versus how little I knew.

But they also inspired me to change and grow.

Thus, in Portland, first I signed up for a class in advertising copy-writing.

Then, more to my situation at the *Journal* and my personal interest, I heard about evening classes at the Portland Art Museum School.

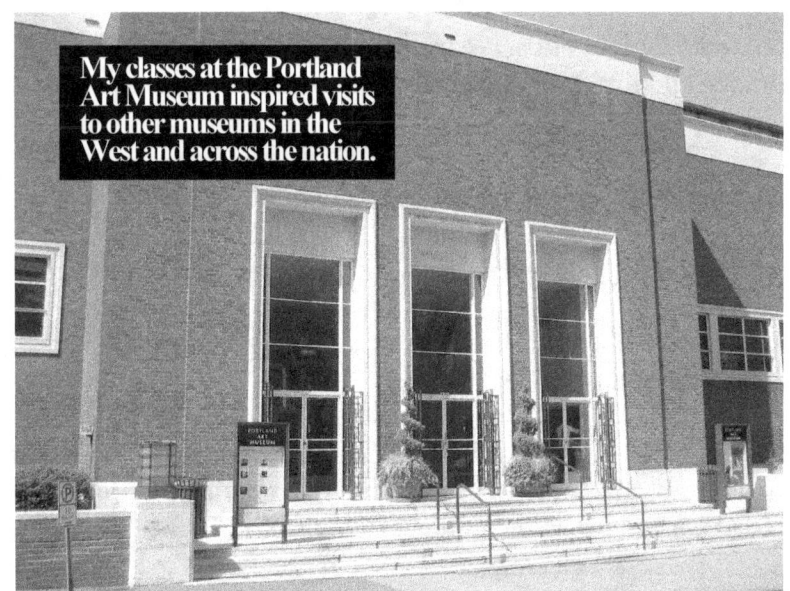

My classes at the Portland Art Museum inspired visits to other museums in the West and across the nation.

The first timely option for me turned out to be a "life drawing" class.

After I overcame the startup shock of a staring at a young woman as a model—nude—my discomfiture faded and I learned about drawing a human.

Da Vinci, I'm on my way!

I'd share a copy of one of my drawings, but—alas—I think my shocked wife destroyed that entire bunch.

Well, I wouldn't want to shock others either!

When that class concluded (sorry to say), I looked to see what class might be available next.

I learned that **calligraphy** related to lettering, and my job included employing a variety of letter forms. In Mankato I had been initiated into rudiments of typography and typesetting and printing.

Why not give calligraphy a whirl?

Well, *whirl* might not serve as the best choice of words, because as a grade-school kid I didn't whirl well with those penmanship swirls.

Remember those? Around and around with overlapping circles.

Bad results? Try the up-and-down zig-zags instead. Or in addition.

Okay, I decided to give calligraphy a whirl, so I signed up (with my poor penmanship).

My next shock—calligraphy students packed the classroom, with many already hard at work practicing their *beautiful writing* (as I learned was the basic meaning of *calligraphy*).

Turns out that our instructor—**Lloyd Reynolds**—ranked as a star "performer" in Portland.

Later I learned that he had also earned a unique accolade by being named in a proclamation by the governor of Oregon: **Calligrapher Laureate of Oregon.**

Though he taught an evening class at the Museum Art School, he primarily taught at Reed College (an elite liberal arts college in Portland).

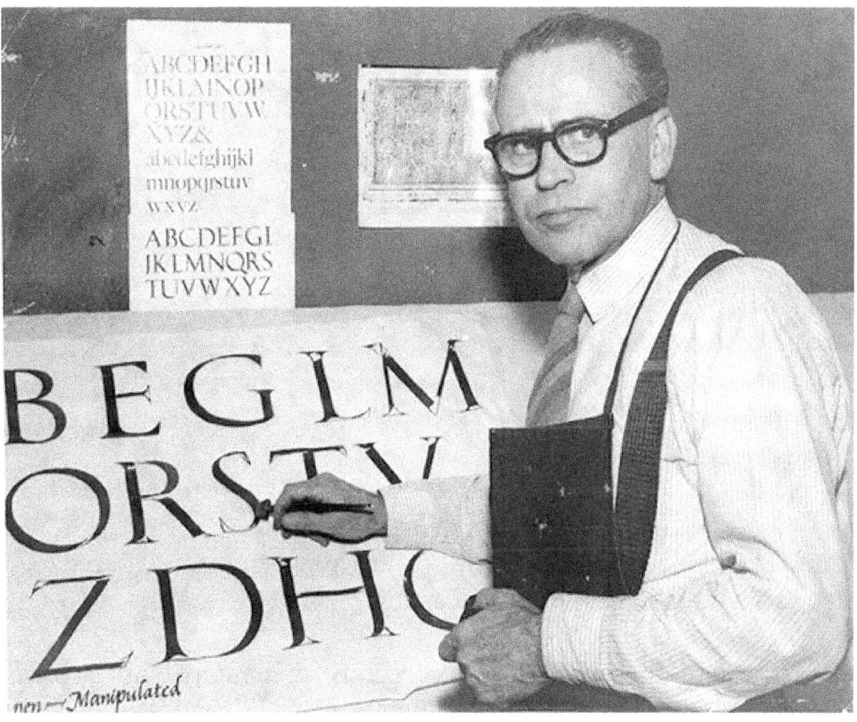

Talk about star power—**Steve Jobs**, among other notables, had studied calligraphy at Reed, and had declared that the study of calligraphy had inspired him to extraordinary dedication about design at Apple. Not to mention his pioneering in the development of computer typography.

So here I was, a neophyte thrust into the swarm of dedicated calligraphers. But I persisted, as I grasped the vital basics.

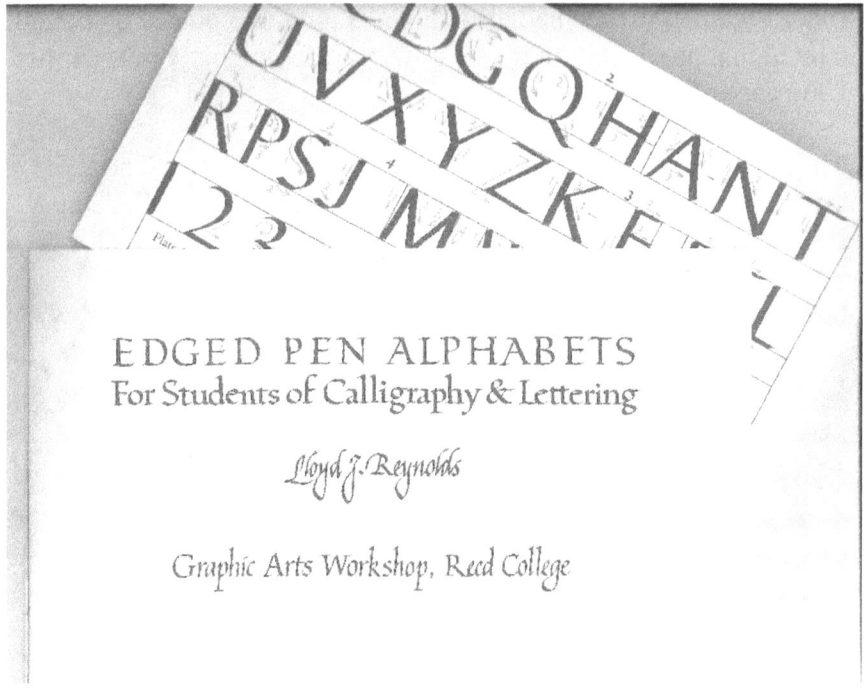

EDGED PEN ALPHABETS
For Students of Calligraphy & Lettering

Lloyd J. Reynolds

Graphic Arts Workshop, Reed College

Some 60 years later, I still refer to Reynolds' collection of charts.

And I've looked at the some of the 20 TV programs he offered to teach via Oregon Public Broadcasting.

Later, when I dropped in on a community calligraphy class to learn about new techniques and materials, I became a "mini-star" as others in the class learned that I had classes from Lloyd Reynolds.

Sorry that I hadn't had a chance to get better acquainted with him, because we should have been simpatico. He also grew up in Minnesota and before teaching he worked in the forest products industry (as I later did with my career of many years with Weyerhaeuser Company).

And I took a fling at teaching calligraphy too. With charts I adapted from the master craftsman!

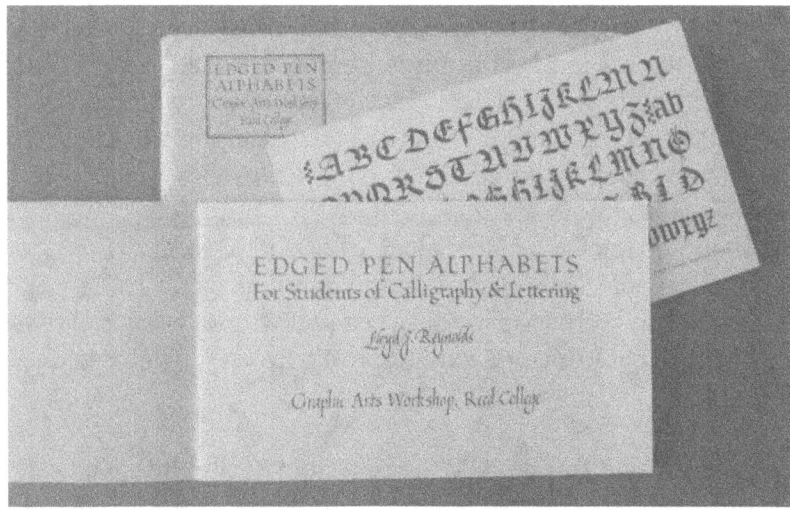

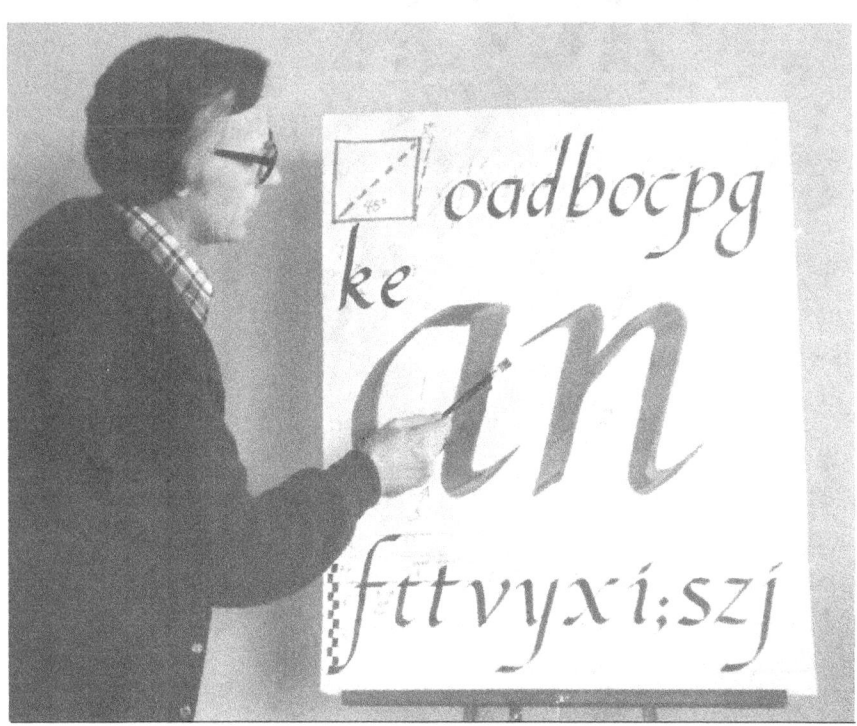

41

Wish I could say that the students I taught in church and community shared the dedication and discipline of the Art Museum students.

Like noted later about The **Bauhaus**, students needed to start from scratch. In a gentle way, I tried to increase their appreciation for the fundamentals (not unlike sports or other disciplines). After all, music students must endure practicing the scales—over and over.

Surprisingly, geometry dictates much of the basic forms of calligraphy, as noted in the chart on the previous page.
Certain angles as well as space between and within letters (known as kerning in typesetting and calligraphy) help establish a basic system.

Don't give up hope for freedom. This system of thin lines and set angles can adapt to change. Such as jamming letters and words together to create a concise, memorable logo for an organization.

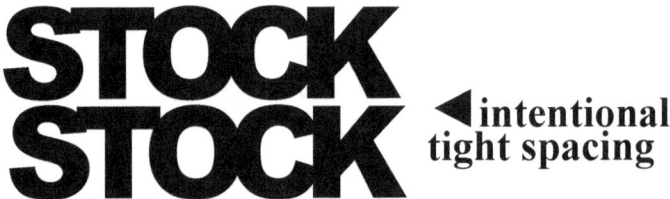

◀ intentional tight spacing

This kind of manipulation of type can produce interesting "ligatures" like above for special purposes. But be wary and keep in mind a primary constraint in calligraphy—the words must be readable!

Regarding readability, the choice of typeface can make a slight—or significant—difference. The face with the serifs that add distinction generally proves move readable. And you won't get confused between the capital "I I" and the lower-case "I l", for instance. But the sans-serif type Helvetica has generated arguments and even became the subject of a movie (type-cast!).

And Helvetica appears as design in many prominent places.

Earlier, in the '30s, The **Bauhaus**, as just mentioned, from Germany, already had led to some significant developments of serif and san-serif type.

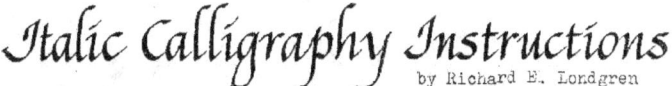

*Italic Calligraphy Instructions*

by Richard E. Londgren

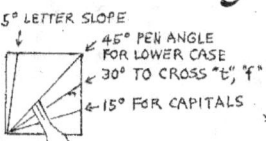

5° LETTER SLOPE

45° PEN ANGLE FOR LOWER CASE
30° TO CROSS "t", "f"
15° FOR CAPITALS

Consistent angles are vital to calligraphy. Lower case letters should be made with the pen at a 45-degree angle. So they are heavier, capitals should be made with a 15-degree angle. When crossing the "t" or "f", change the angle to 30 degrees.

Italic letters should slope slightly--about 5 degrees from the vertical.

abcdefghijklmnopqrstuvwxyz
ABCDEFGHIJKLMNOPQRS
TUVWXYZ 1234567890

Height relationships are also important. Distance from the top of lower case ascenders to the bottom of descenders is equal to 15 pen widths. Note the lower height of capitals and numbers. Letters can be made heavier by decreasing the height.

Space in and between letters varies for pleasing appearance. Capitals and numbers are proportionally wider than lower case. Note the contrast between the small and capital "o". Leave less space next to a curved or open letter, such as "a" or "c", than a straight one.

oacedb

The "o" is a basic shape that is part of these and other letters.

abcdefghijklmnopqrstuvwxyz &
A B C D E F G H I J K L M N O P
Q R S T U V W X Y Z 123456789

Connecting letters in the cursive form and adding flourishes can increase the beauty of the calligraphy, but don't allow excessive ornamentation to impair the readability of the words.

Still, the basic system of fundaments will serve as a foundation and allow for adding flow and flourish.

The italic form on the previous page sets one standard with its distinctive letters and numbers set at a 5-degree slant. The angles in some other letters change, as in the bolder example shown below.

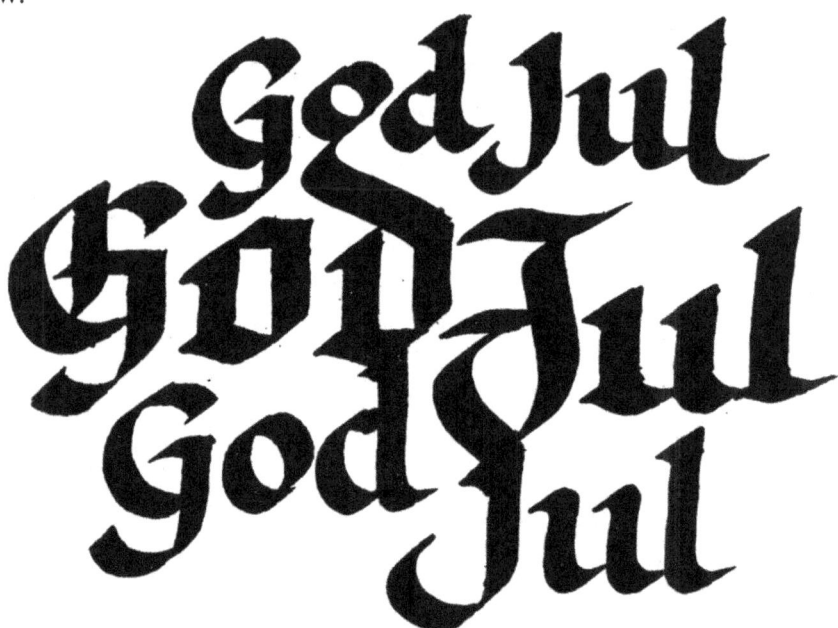

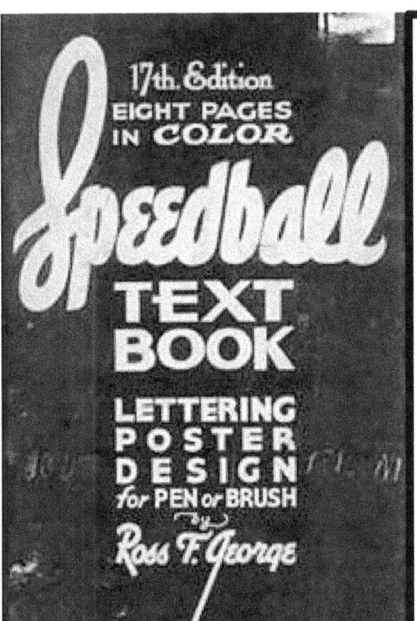

Some students have learned their lettering from this book by Speedball, which features letters from graceful to garish.

This lettering guide does include a wide range of letters. And sometimes bold and blatant can serve a need, as noted here elsewhere as it relates to my book called *Communication by Objectives*.

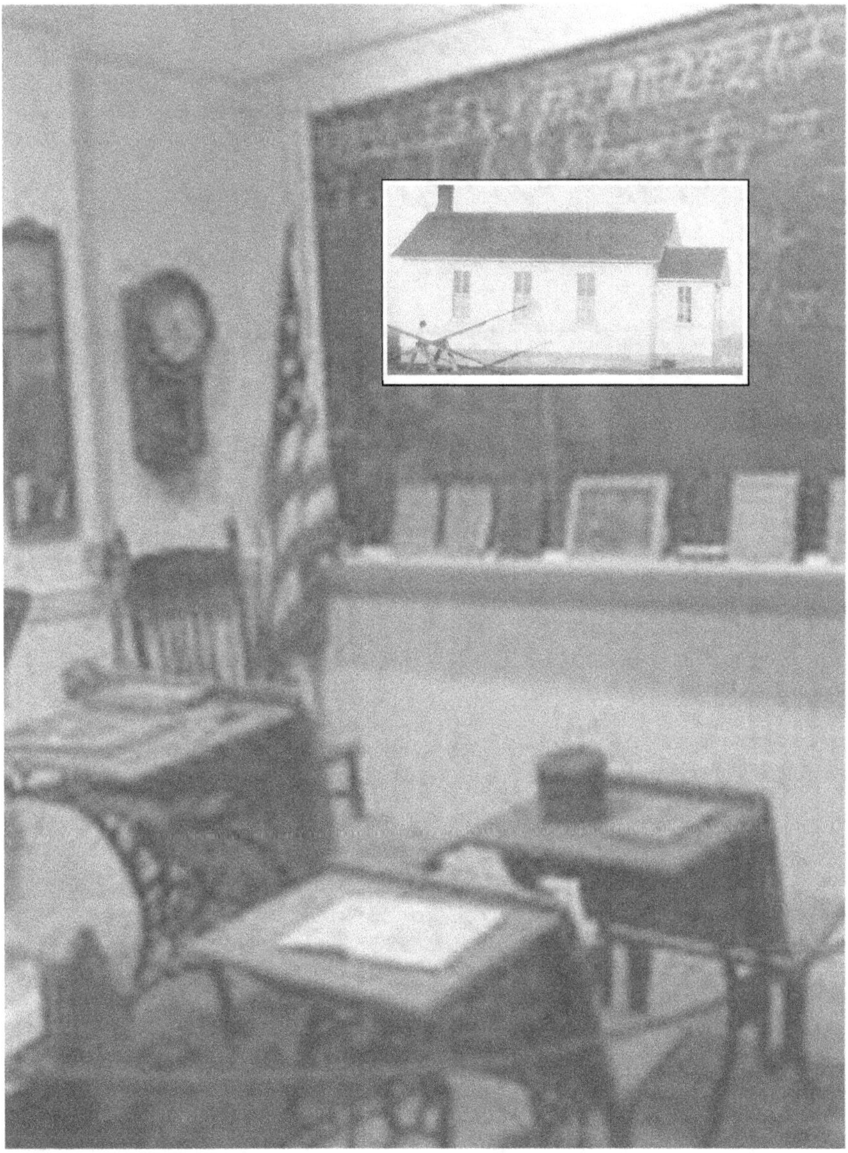

If you went to a Country School like I did for a short time, you'll probably remember the letter examples like those shown here at the top of the blackboard. But in my "more-sophisticated" town-school later, we learned our letters from an "exquisite" set of printed letters—probably from the Palmer Method of penmanship as shown on the next page.

*Palmer*

*A B C D E F G*

*H I J K L M N O*

*P Q R S T U V*

*W X Y Z a b c d e f*

*g h i j k l m n o p q*

*r s t u v w x y z 1 2*

# Creating a Logo

# STOCK
# STOCK

In Microsoft Word or Publisher, on the **Font** category, this all-caps 48 pt. Arial Black type was condensed by 7.8 pt. to run the letters together and still be readable.

On the **Paragraph** category, **multiple** lines of type were set at spacing of .65 pica to bring the lines of type as close as practical without distortion.

This method could be applied to create a LOGO in all caps, but lower-case letters would require more-careful handling.

# Stock
# Stock

For suitable readable spacing of lower-case letters, the condensed **font** of the second word was set at 5.7 pt. instead of 7.8 pt. in the first word.

LIFE and LOOK magazines both began (in the modern form for LIFE) in the mid-'30s, and both feature the short and strong logos made of all-caps.

However, the spacing of the letters of LIFE could have benefited from some tweaking, with the "I" closer to the "L" and separated a bit more from the "F."

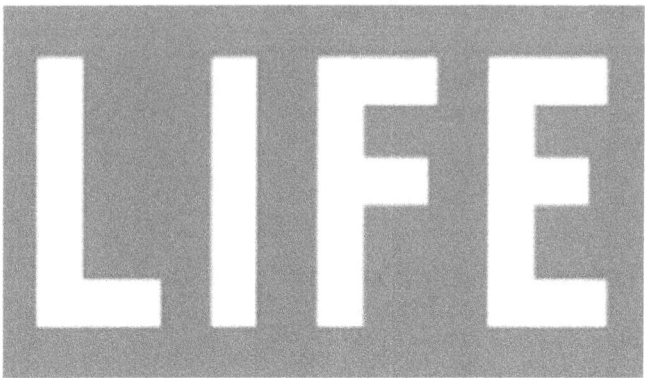

And the letters of LOOK also feature all-caps that could have "looked" more interesting if kerned to overlap while still being readable. But that was then, and this is now!

Still, BAUHAUS might have offered such advice then.

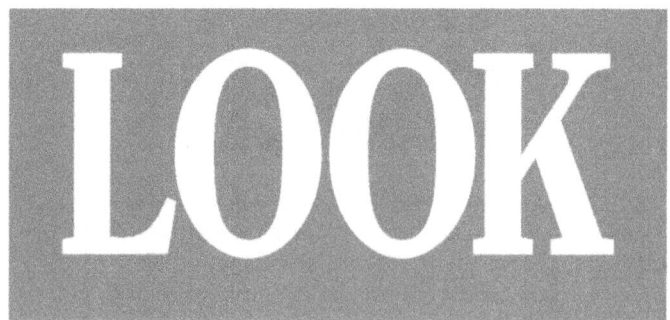

# Toolz of the Trade

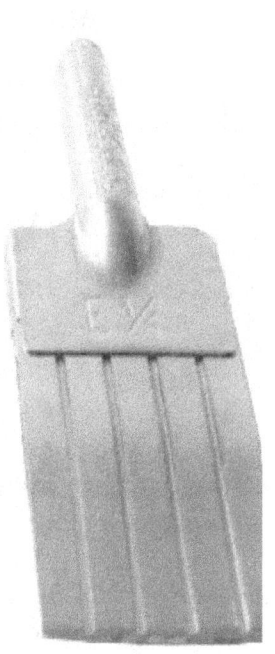

As in other "trades," calligraphy tools can be specific or general purpose.

So here we go again with Speedball for many pens, including the steel brush at left. This ¾"-wide broad "brush" gives gusto as well as delicacy to your letters. (Lefties, Speedball makes pens for you too.)

Sharpie offers chisel-point pens (look later at my example of the Sharpies I use for convenience and fast action) and now Sharpies include a "magnum" that is also 3/4" wide.

For practice, use a carpenter's wide pencil. Sharpen with a knife and some sandpaper.

When lettering with this "lead," press hard…on paper with some texture. That can create an interesting effect.

And try making your own pens. When I needed a ¼" pen, I decided to make one out of a clock spring. With wood handle. It works—sort of. Sharpened bamboo is another option. And consider a chisel-shaped sponge-brush for large sign work.

Ink also varies for purpose and color. Lots of stiff brushes work well, with tempera and acrylic paint.

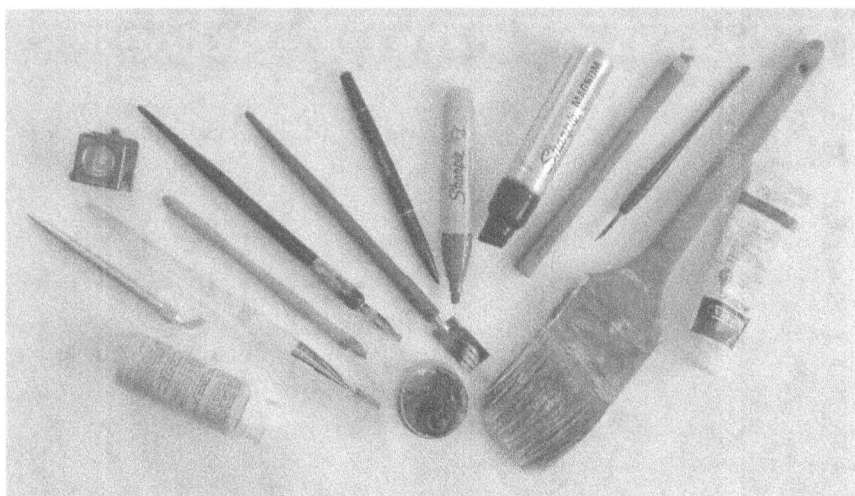

A drawing board, T-square and triangle will help with alignment of the letters. For marking big posters, I even made a T-square with a long blade, to run along the edge of a large tablet or a table.

Programs on the Internet offer helpful guidance about tools and techniques. My Facebook called **Richard Londgren Books** includes links to demonstrations, including information by and about Lloyd Reynolds.

The same for information about type and printing—from letterpress to 3-D printing.

To simplify church internal publicity about new members, I letter the name of the member on a form to be held for identification. In fact, the subjects and I often joke about the holding of an ID.

But with the name in the photo, the photo can be displayed on the bulletin board and reproduced with the name in the newsletter.

But remember—keep it simple when you can.

I often used lined bookkeeping paper (surplus) for this purpose, and I letter with a chisel-point Sharpie. I call my improvised type **Baltic Bold**. See examples later.

For checking details, more likely for typography than calligraphy, I also keep a magnifier handy, including the printer's **thread-counter** for closeup magnifying.

Color guides too. First printed charts, now on the computer as well.

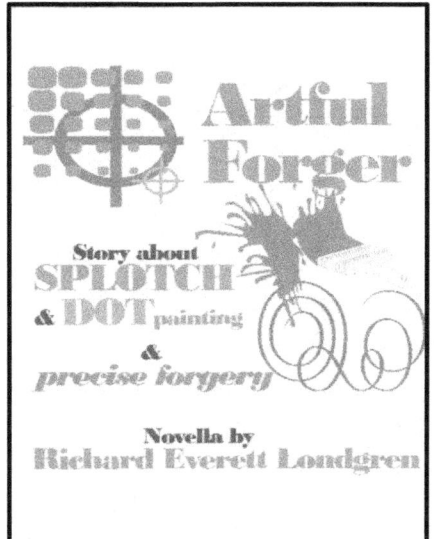

In my story *Artful Forger*, the high school "muralist" painted a large scene high up on the sawmill wall and used his own *pointillism* of "splotches and dots" to create an image.

To view the effect of his pointillism from his vantage, he placed a large salvaged mirror some distance away to check his results.

Thus, in the small scale of the distant mirror, he got the "big picture" of his splotches and dots produced pointillistic painting.

And at the time of my writing, I wondered about the "mirror writing" by da Vinci.

Did he actually use a mirror, or even his camera obscura, to achieve that effect?

Evidently, he used mirror writing to conceal, not reveal.

When I did finally look up information about mirror writing, I learned that such ability comes from the brain in a few persons, which converts images like a mirror.

And only a select few can turn that on.

Meanwhile, I try to use my left hand as well as right for many functions—starting mainly when I was a kid with hope for hoops in basketball by becoming ambidextrous.

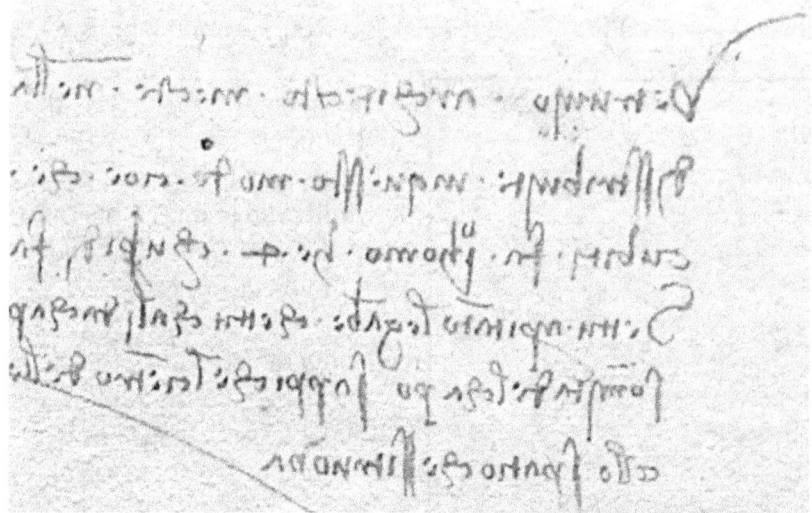

I can at least do some primitive calligraphy with my left as well —not quite as well—as with my right.

But not a mirror image, as in da Vinci's example above.

Well, there's no one quite like da Vinci!

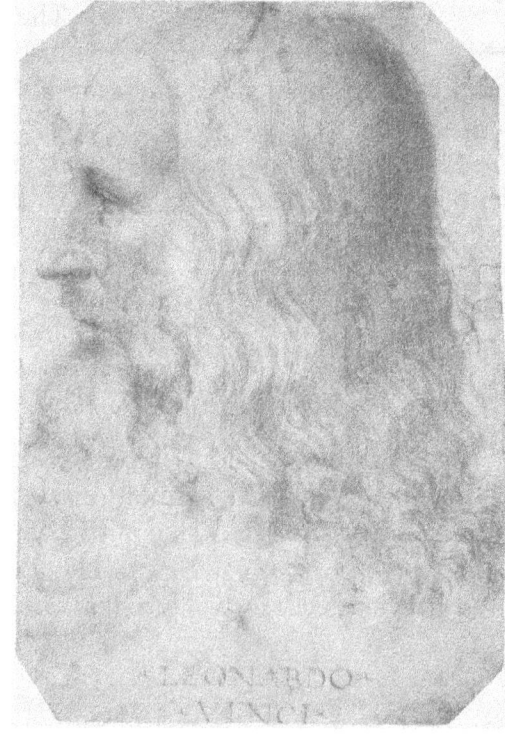

# Portland ▶ Tacoma

When I realized I was stalled in my job at the *Journal,* I sought the advice from my boss about my future. As this calligraphy indicates, I didn't know whether I was coming or going. So, he frankly counseled me that I should consider going to college full time, rather than haphazard part-time courses. And he suggested art and architecture, though he personally recommended liberal arts study. He spoke from experience, because he said that route had served him well in career and life.

After further recommendations from my associates, I also sought the advice of my Lutheran pastor in Portland. Not surprisingly, he recommended Pacific Lutheran College in Tacoma, Washington—the only Lutheran four-year college in the West.

I wrote for information, then followed up with a visit there. It seemed right for me. Size. Even the cost, for a private school. And I had finally saved some money to consider attending. So I was accepted. And I enrolled. College at last, after my several early hopeless years!

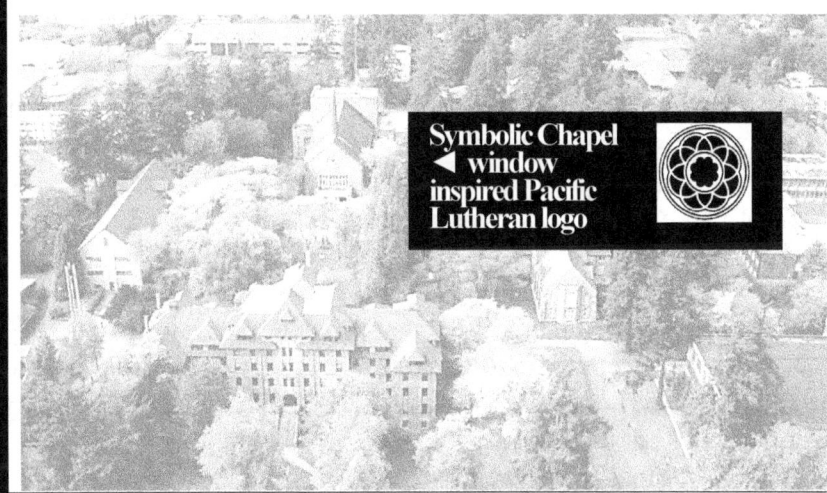

Symbolic Chapel ◀ window inspired Pacific Lutheran logo

So here I was, still in the lush Pacific Northwest, with a different

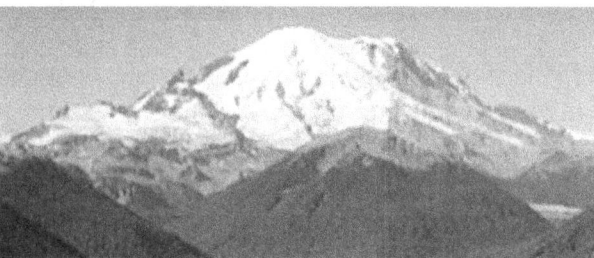

view—this time Mt. Rainier.

But my earlier experience paid off, as I became art editor of the college yearbook and I designed and wrote for the student newspaper. I eventually became the editor. Lots of late-night work—but no pay or credit.

For work/study, I earned and learned in the public relations department, helping with graphics, writing, publications and setting up meetings. I also worked with Tacoma and Seattle printers.

Then, between summer-school classes and before starting as editor of the student newspaper, I created a handbook to organize for the editing challenge. Practical, valuable knowledge.

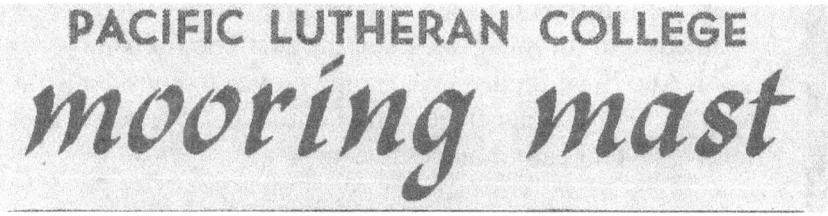

PACIFIC LUTHERAN COLLEGE
*mooring mast*

Talk about primitive printing. I prepared a stencil for the cover (even managed to scribe on the stencil a calligraphy-style copy of the new calligraphed nameplate I had created for the newspaper). Remember the purple "Ditto" printing once used by teachers? I "Ditto-d" the inside pages and added a sample page of headline styles printed by a local printer for reference.

I did get extra college credit for that project. That, along with maximizing the hours I could take each semester (at no extra cost) and taking summer classes, I was able to finish college in three years (Shock! at the top of my class). Saved money and allowed me to move quickly back into the workforce and earn some pay.

At last! After my nose to the grindstone with continual work and study.

But before I finished as editor, the *Mooring Mast* did announce a special engagement—after I proposed to **Anita Hillesland**, a college senior from San Francisco. And she accepted marriage to this bumpkin from the tiny town of Lynd, Minnesota (remember, population 218, dwarfed by the 718-**thousand** of San Francisco).

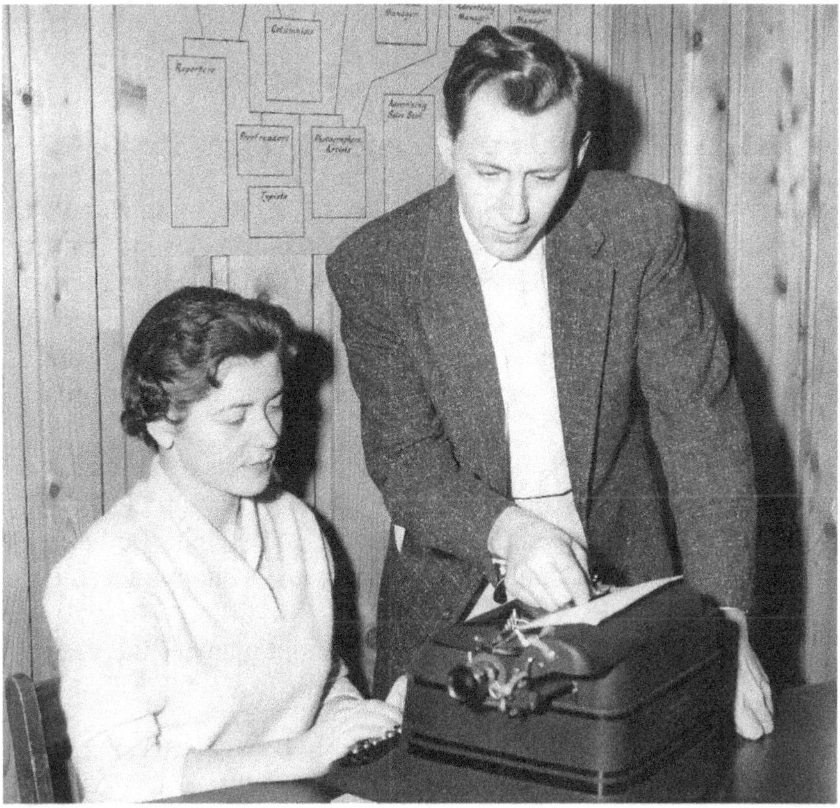

**MOORING MAST EDITORS,** present and future, discuss part of a story for the last Mooring Mast of the semester. Anita Hillesland was named by the PLC literary board as editor of the paper during the spring semester. The retiring editor, Dick Londgren, will graduate at the end of this semester.

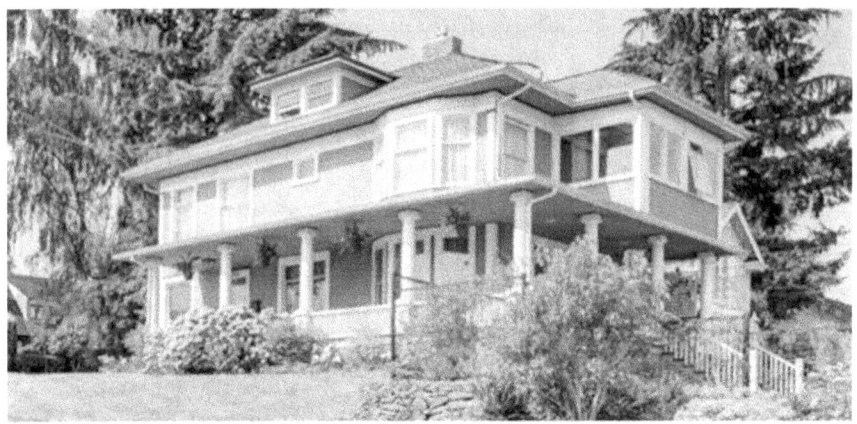

# SignZ of the changing TimeZ
Trinity
After we were married in San Francisco at Anita's home church,
Trinity Lutheran, we temporarily rented a house close to Pacific
Lutheran in Parkland. Then we bought a small house in nearby
Lakewood. Next, we discovered the older North End of Tacoma
and purchased the house shown above, which we lived in and
worked on for nearly 40 years. And raised our three kids there.

With our kids grown and new options open to us, we moved to
the four-bedroom house shown below in Thousand Oaks,
California. Within walking distance to Holy Trinity Lutheran
Church, California Lutheran University and a shopping center.

The next pages will fill in the blanks about many of the years
and our activities along the way.

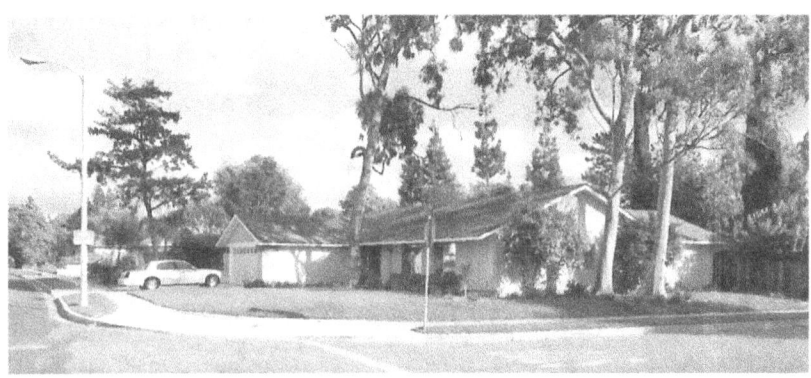

# Corporate Career

After college, I landed on my feet. Or my feet landed on the land, because I joined the publications and public relations department ot the huge forestland company, Weyerhaeuser.

But it was known as Weyerhaeuser Timber Company when I went to work in the Tacoma headquarters.

Weyerhaeuser

Eventually, after the company shortened the name and added the triangular symbol, I served as the point-man (sometimes jokingly called the Corporate Identity Czar) responsible for assuring proper use of the logo on signs and vehicles and packaging…and anything that might bear the name.

Once again, I benefited from ongoing learning. From my well-educated and experienced collegues and from the advertising and graphics agencies I worked with. And from the big printing firms that produced our publications—including one major printer in Portland.

At the time I joined Weyerhaeuser, a Tacoma office building served as the heaquarters. Later, the headquarters shifted to the dramatic building shown below. Later still, it moved to inner-city Seattle.

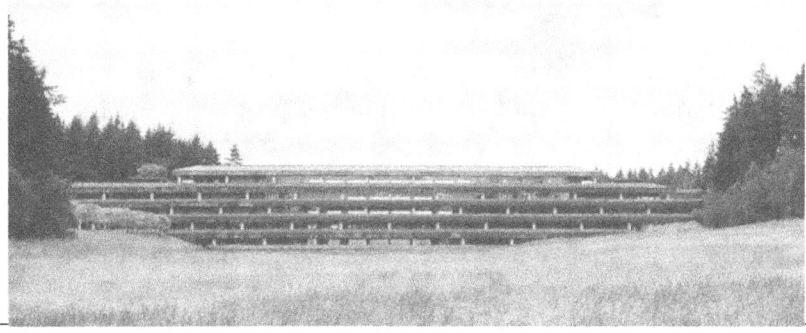

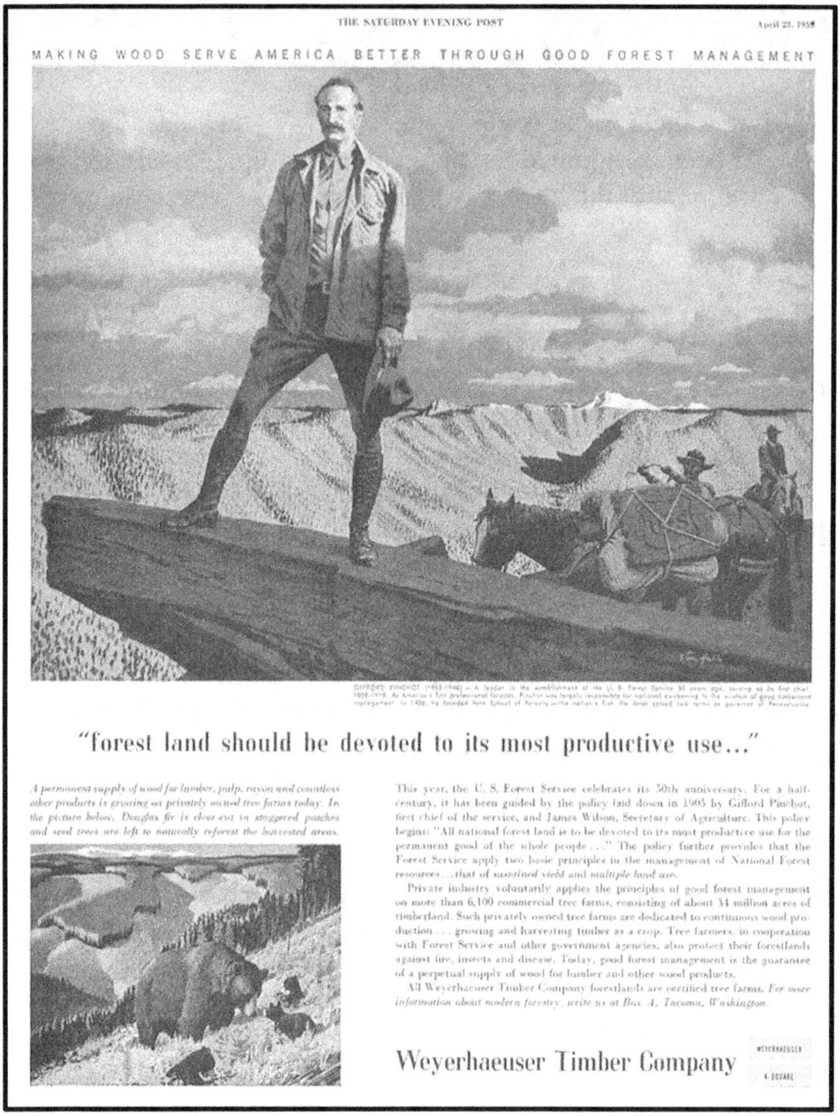

From the start, the Weyerhaeuser national advertising promoted the importance of planning, planting and protecting the forest resource, as shown in this early ad. The birds and animals featured in the long-running campaign caught reader attention and were also used in the popular "wildlife calendars" distributed for many years by the company...until the role of calendars faded with changes in communication.

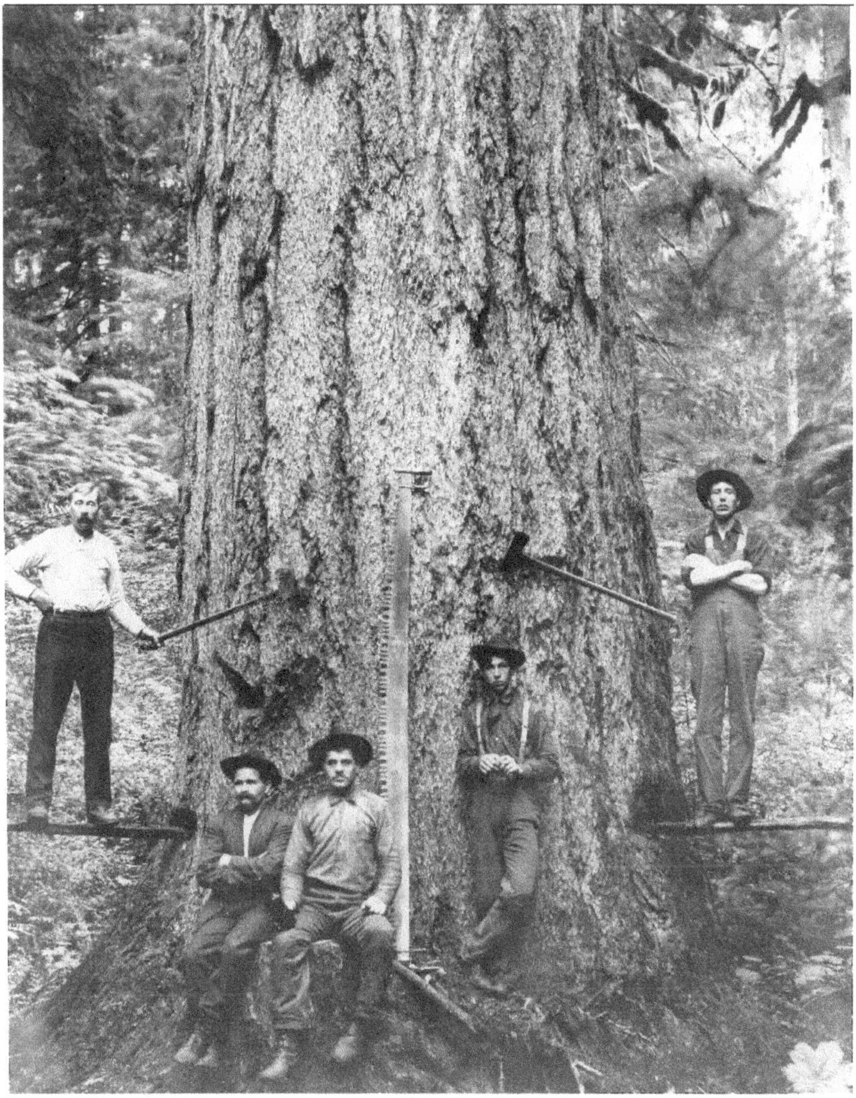

Scenes of logging like this occurred before my association with the forest products industry, but this kind of history stuck in the memory (or imagination) of countless others—especially those opposed to harvesting of any trees.

That impression and attitude set the stage for Weyerhaeuser's noted advertising campaign featuring appealing illustrations like the example on the next page. I even met with some of the artists commissioned for what became popular and informative ads.

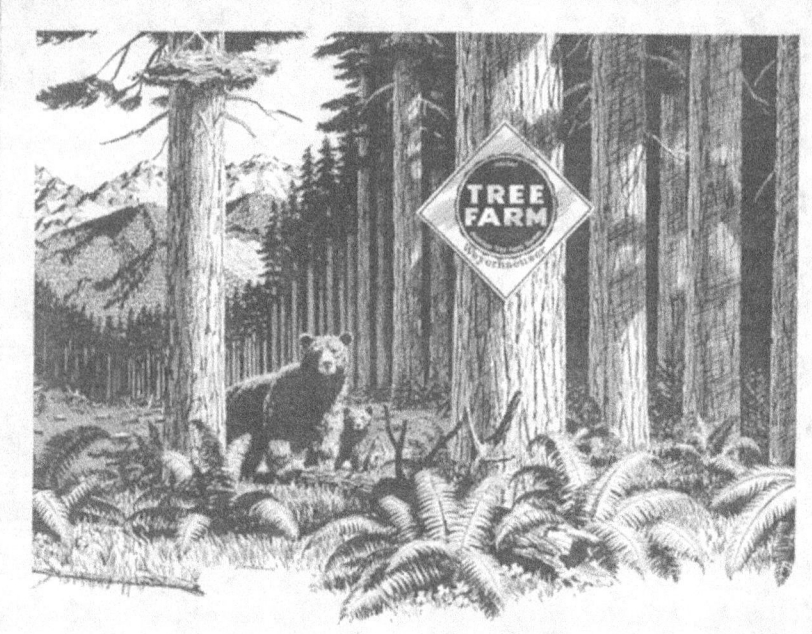

## How tree farming helped save our nation's forests.

Back in 1941, there were fears that the U. S. might run out of trees. And with good reason. The nation was using up 20% more wood than was being grown.

Then Weyerhaeuser helped spark an historic turn-around when we established this country's first tree farm near Montesano, Washington.

Since then more than 31,000 tree farms have been certified under the American tree farm system by private owners everywhere. They cover about 68 million acres of tax-paying land. Under the tree farm concept, the owners agree to grow timber as a crop and protect their forests against fire, insects and disease.

The result: The nation is now growing 61% more wood than is harvested.

This means there can be ample supply of raw material for paper, packaging, building materials and scores of other wood products you use every day. In addition, the trees will continually provide watersheds, wildlife shelters and beautiful recreation areas. If you'd like to know more about the value of tree farms to our nation, write us at Box A-36, Tacoma, Washington 98401. Ask for "Tree Farms to You."

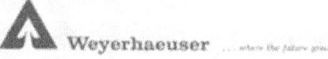 **Weyerhaeuser** ... where the future grows

Though most of Weyerhaeuser's national magazine ads appeared in color, this version adapted to newspapers, even in the small towns with Weyerhaeuser operations. Later, the company advertised on TV, including a sponsorship of 1976 Olympics. So that provided me the opportunity to attend the Olympics for one day in Montreal. I used my photo at right in my book *Communication by Objectives* to relate the Olympics to the use of propaganda, as by Hitler 40 years earlier.

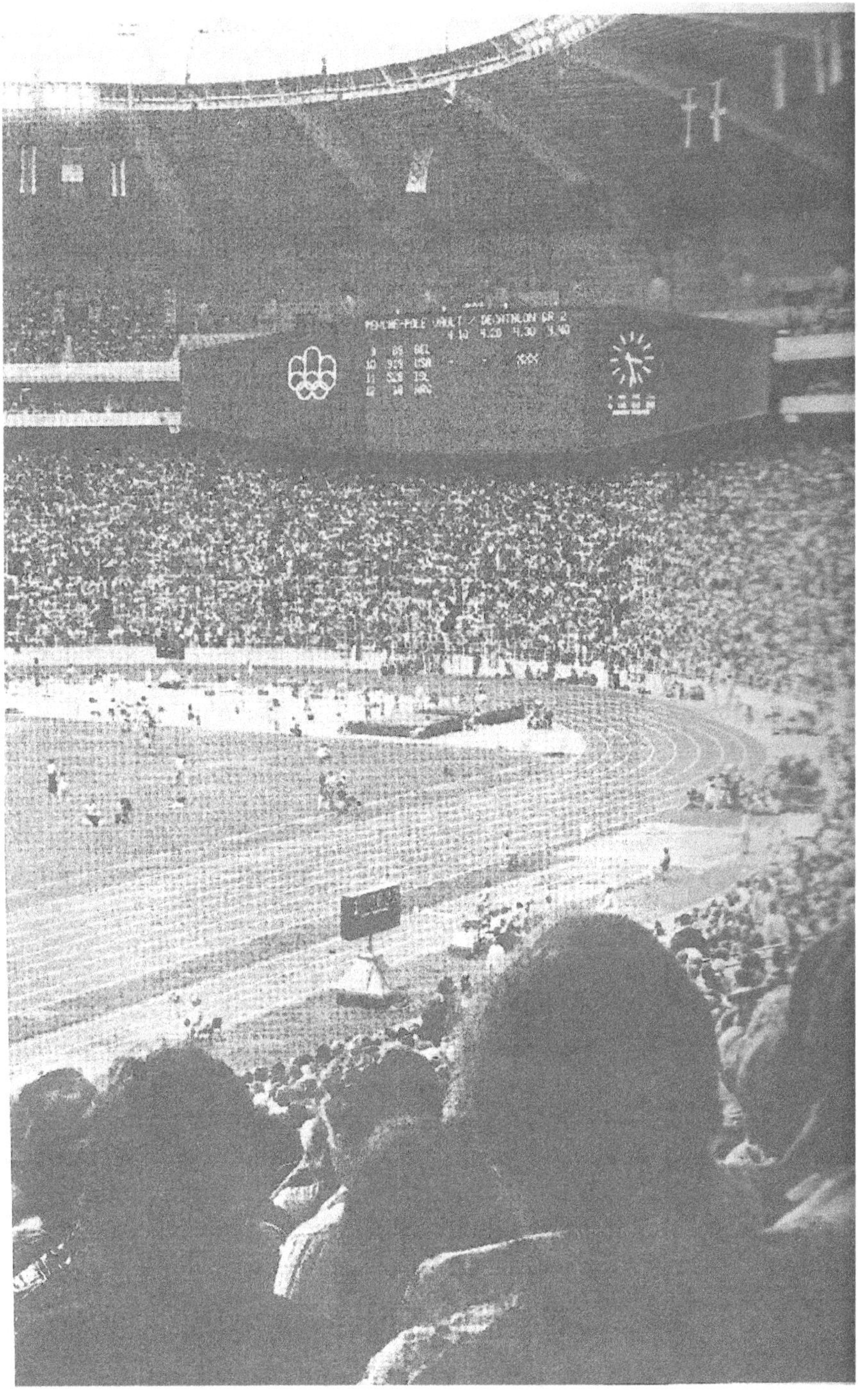

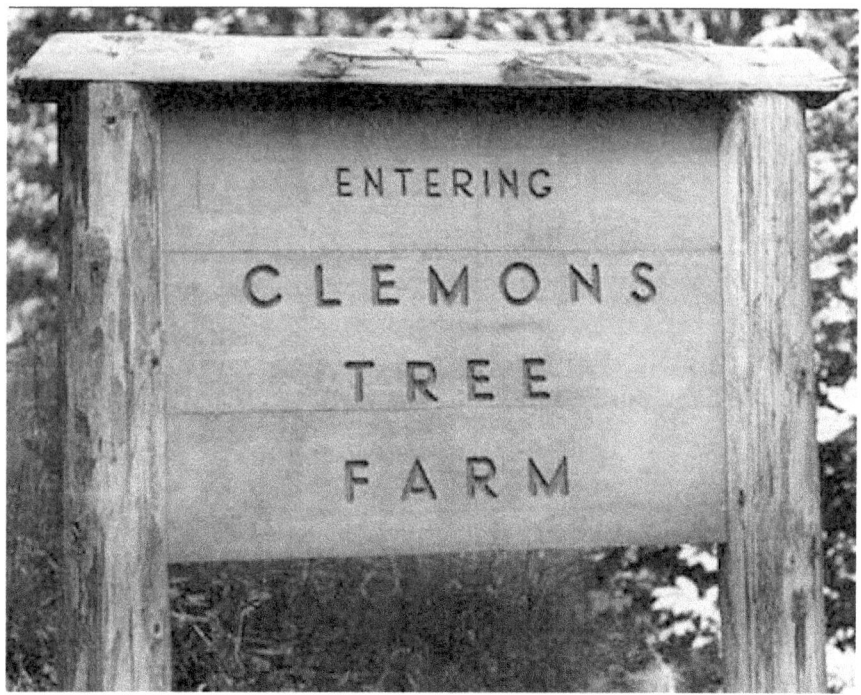

ENTERING

C L E M O N S

T R E E

F A R M

This rustic sign fit an early phase of the Tree Farm program of harvesting and replanting trees, from nursery stock suited to the soil, elevation and other considerations.

Meanwhile, working with the 3M sign division and a Seattle supplier of plastic "appliques," we began a more-contemporary style of sign.

And a different way to indicate the age of a young forest. The new signs, with the Weyerhaeuser logo, simply gave the date the trees were planted.

Go figure! The date matched against the growth of the new trees surprised—astounded!—many skeptics. Just as visitors to the headquarters couldn't imagine that the imposing trees there flourished as part of the third forest because the previous two forests had been harvested.

As in other farming, the planning and planting had to suit the situation for the best results from a new crop.

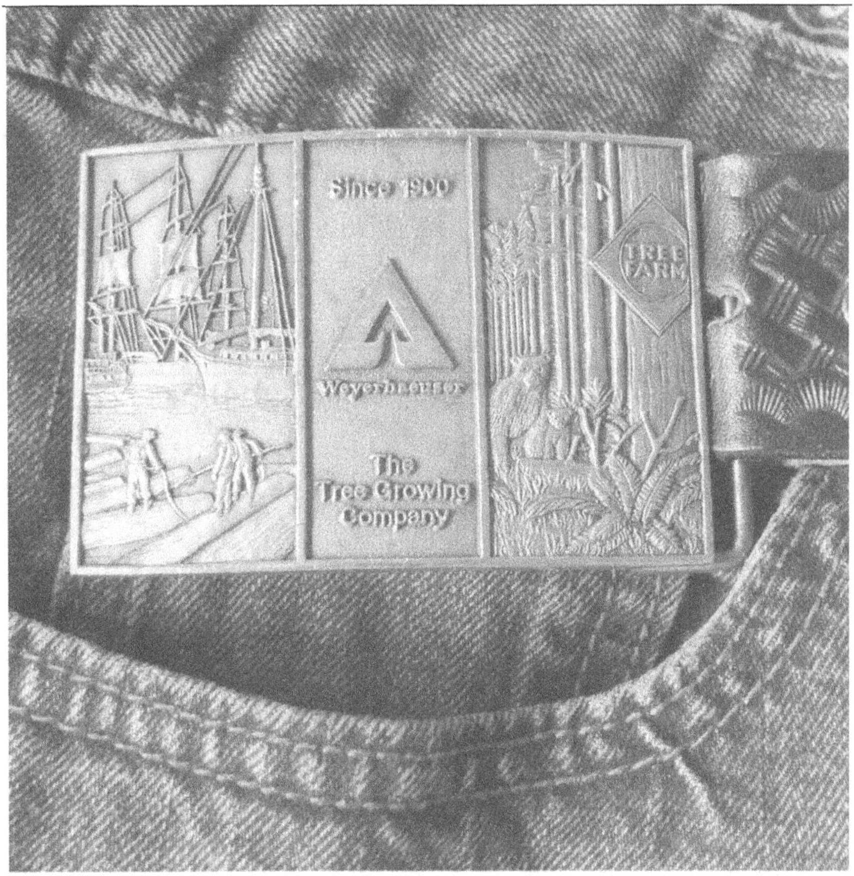

Despite the reality that the Weyerhaeuser name challenged spelling and pronouncing, the name gained recognition from a mix of advertising, including this distinct belt-buckle with scenes as well as the name built in.

A variety of other **tangible advertising** featured "wearable advertising" such as hats and clothes as well as promotion on pens and everyday items to spread the company's name and message.

Signs on vehicles, buildings and in the forests as well as the local, regional and national advertising increased the visibility of the name and accompanying symbol, which one critic called a contradiction—removing the word "Timber" from the name but then putting a tree in the triangular symbol.

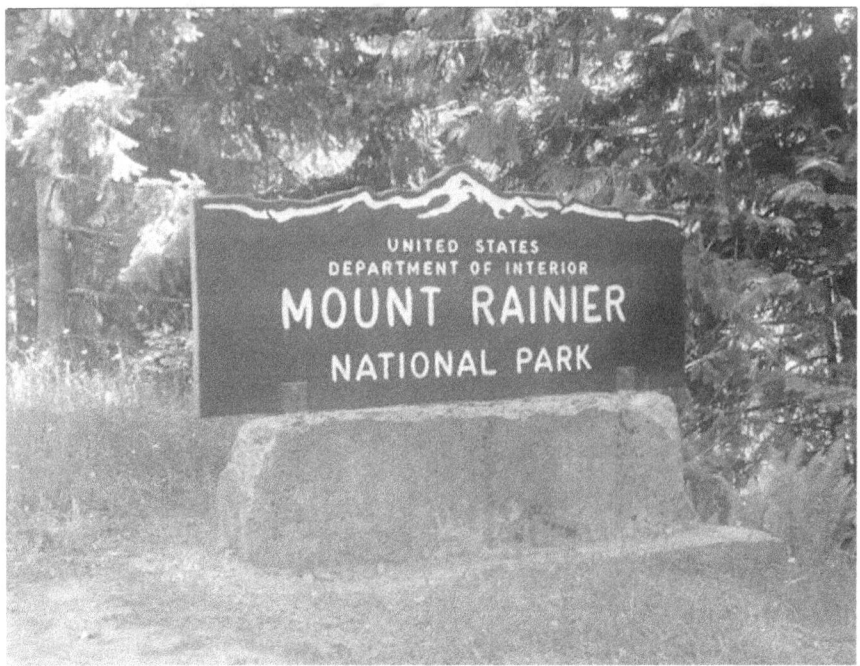

From the earliest days of our country, signs have served as a vital role in communication.

In the national park system, signs proliferate with usual information and warnings.

Ben Franklin told the story of editing a hat-maker's sign. As a conclusion from increasing input of opinions, the "advisors" declared that just a symbolic shape of a hat would suffice. No words needed.

Even in a wilderness park near our home, a sign with a drawing of a rattlesnake would certainly get your attention.

The state drivers' manual reminds us what to look for in the various standard road signs.

And it pays to review those before taking your driver's test, because a near-miss in identification might require you to come back to take the test again to pass.

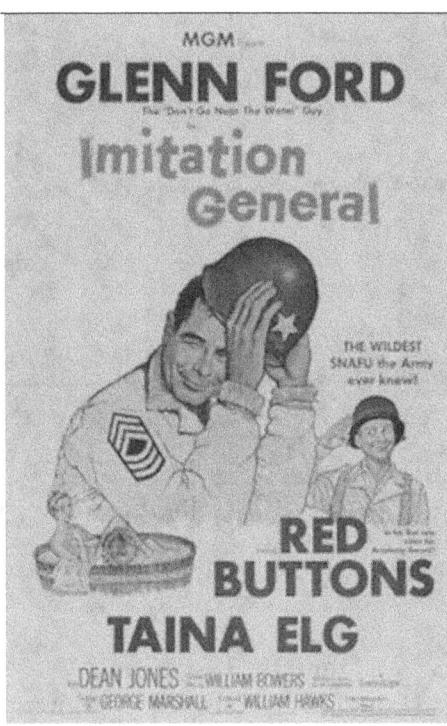

The movie with Glenn Ford starring as the enlisted man who became the *Imitation General* demonstrated the imaginative use of a sign. Recognizing the "rules of the road," the imitation general realized that the German tank-drivers would avoid a bridge with a sign declaring it unsafe because of mines.

When diverted to crossing in the streambed, the tanks made easy targets as they emerged up the bank.

Of course, **Hollywood** also produced a world-famous sign with that name staked out letter-by-letter on the hillside near Griffith Park.

What began as a real estate promotion has turned into an icon of California.

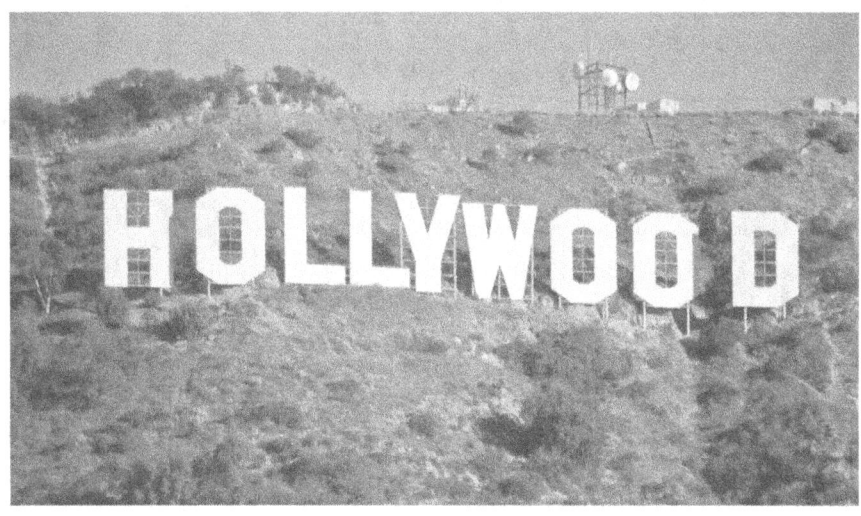

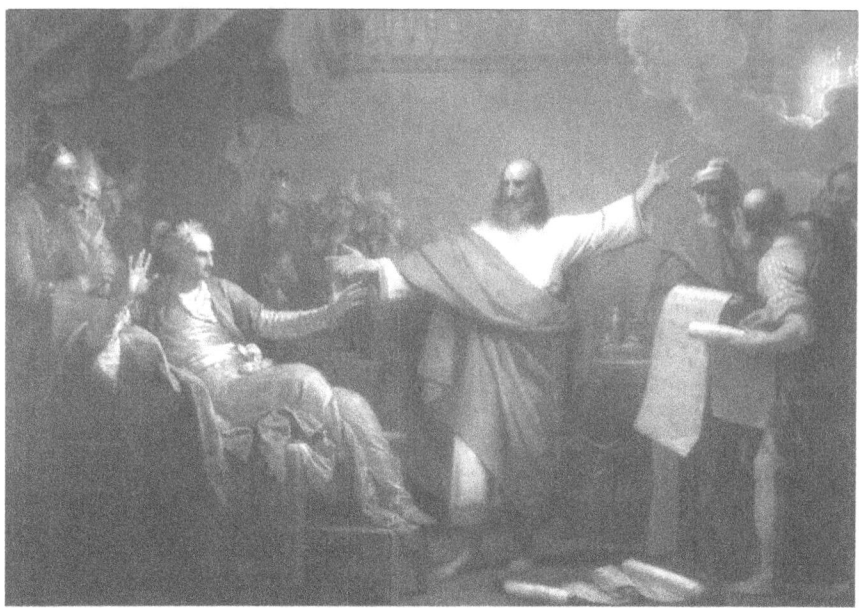

The Bible exceeds Hollywood, because this Old Testament challenge by **Rembrandt** depicts **Daniel** interpreting the "writing on the wall." Risky, because what Daniel read was not well received. So, off to the lions with Daniel. But God came to the rescue.

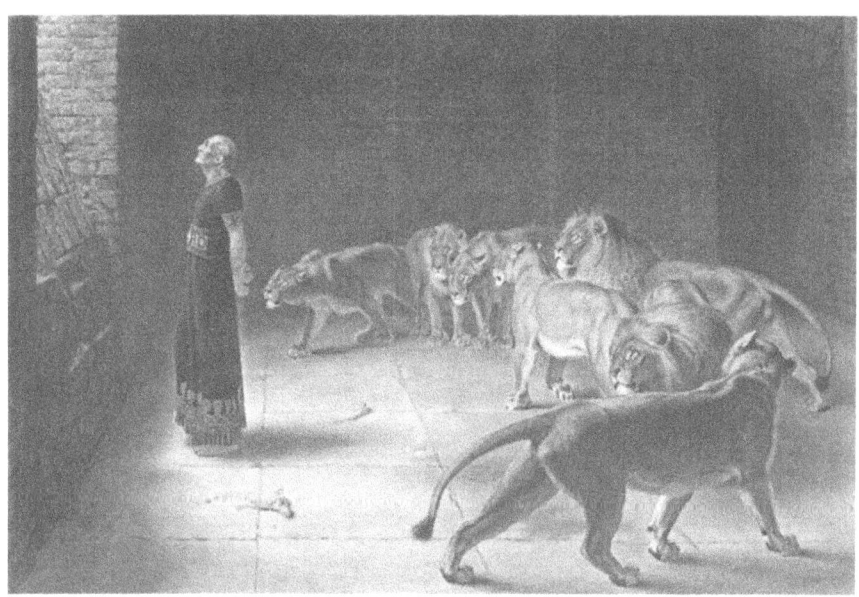

# Employee Growth

Weyerhaeuser, like most contemporary organizations, bets on its people as well as on its trees. Training opportunities benefited many in our offices, forests and mills.

Tapping into programs provided by organizations such as the American Management Association, a wide range of managers had access to learning opportunities. And networking with others with similar interests and challenges.

That applied to staff departments as well, including our public relations, publications and graphics department.

All participation was subject to department/company budgeting and endorsement and approval, of course.

Selected persons in key positions might even go on leave to pursue an advanced degree or go on loan to another non-competing company or, rarely, become a White House Fellow.

I didn't make it to the White House (except as a tourist) by appointment or election.

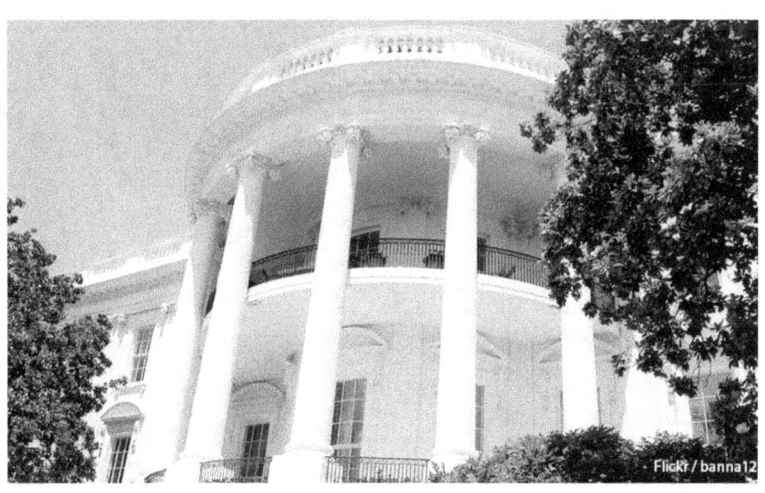

Flickr / banna12

But almost every year I did take in a class or workshop related to my responsibilities. Often that provided a chance to visit an agency or supplier of interest to our department and our company. When I served on a national church communication board, that included opportunity for special training and interaction as well.

Through my reporting assignments for the company-wide news-magazine, I visited many locations of our manufacturing facilities and those of important customers. And I went to Hollywood once, for instance, to report about a company product being used in the movies. That time—not a typical situation—the movie publicist arranged for me have lunch at the same table as Red Buttons (who chatted but concentrated mostly on his script for *Imitation General* as mentioned earlier). James Garner sat a few tables away. Next I met Richard Chamberlain, suiting up for his Dr. Kildare medical role at the time.

Later, we had a more-direct link to Hollywood. Our daughters worked for movie studios and our son-in-law is a movie publicist.

On my own, I also learned while teaching at four colleges, including an evening for-credit class in public relations at the University of Washington. There I benefited also from association with my amazing students—from top graphics companies, *The Seattle Times* and advertising agencies. They came not for a degree, but for enrichment and networking.

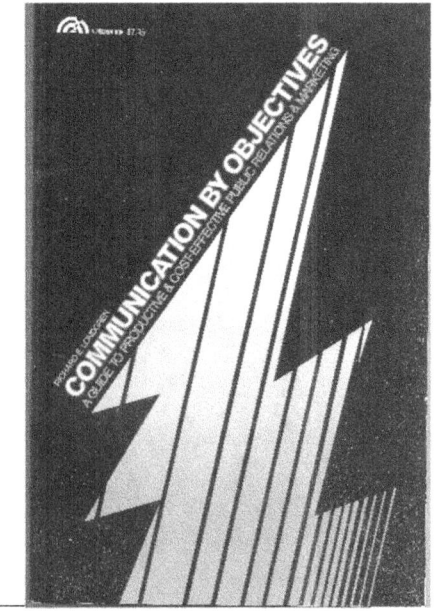

Out of that class came an inquiry from Prentice-Hall about my writing a book about my class in *Communication by Objectives.*

Four challenging years later, I picked up my first copies at the Prentice-Hall printing plant in New Jersey, across the Hudson River from Manhattan.

# Start the PresseZ!

In a surprise opportunity, I suddenly got a chance to acquire an antique platen press. As if I needed more "opportunities" to add to the steady repair required for our recently-purchased 1906 four-story house.

But ever since I saw such a press in action in our town of Lynd, I nursed a hankering for such a press. With far more hankering than hands-on skill or knowledge.

But a friend who knew of my hankering alerted me to a 2,200-pound, six-foot-high Chandler & Price press with a 12" x 18" platen.

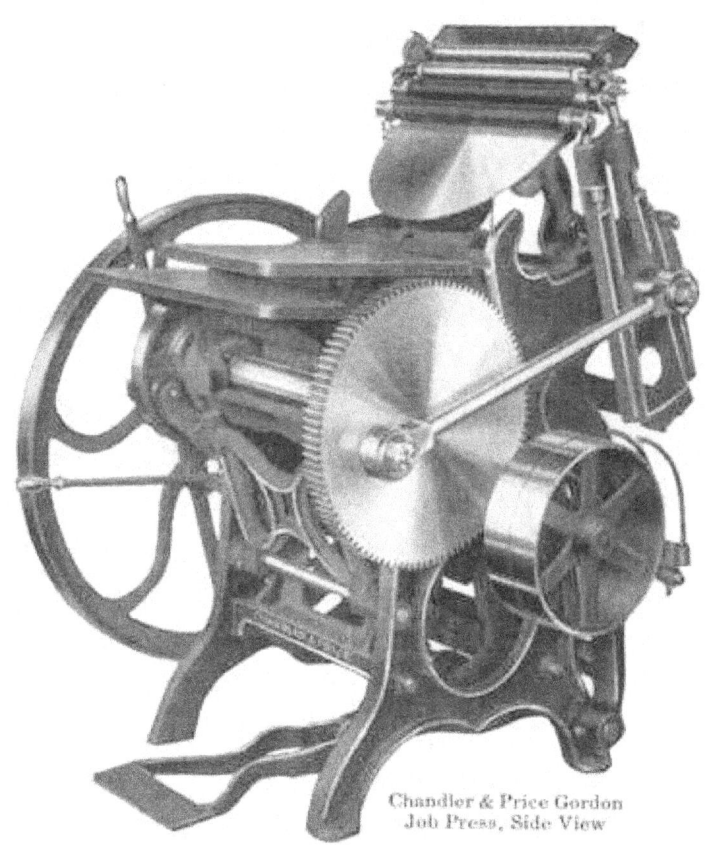

Chandler & Price Gordon
Job Press, Side View

We hadn't time or priority to repair our ramshackle garage with its floor of broken-up concrete.

But now or never at the bargain price! With lots of goodies too, such as drawers of type, forms, furniture, tools, ink.

I borrowed an industrial rolling-jack, rented a truck with a power lift-gate and brought pipes as rollers. Off I went to meet some helpers at the printing plant.

We managed to move the press onto the tailgate, as the truck strained to lift the load. Then we positioned the rolling-jack in place to move the press inside the truck. Next, the composing table, plus type drawer by drawer. Then smaller stuff. And off to drive 10 miles to our house.

With planks on the broken concrete in the garage, we unloaded the press (again with strain on the truck lift-gate) into the garage. With a tarp over all the equipment, we called it a day. And I spent months more repairing the garage roof and creating a seven-foot-wide room for the printshop.

My brother and I poured concrete in that printshop. After due time, we used pipes on planks to roll the press into place in the shop.

Eventually, we poured concrete in the rest of the garage and repaired doors and windows. And the garage area even held our small car! There's more, such as restoring the wiring—but that's all the gory details for now.

Just take my word for it—I did finally take the press for a trial-and-error run. Slowly I learned the ropes, and I learned that this kind of printing offers challenges far beyond even primitive graphics involving the old cut-and-paste preparation for printing.

But now I needed to name my press (mine, because my wife and kids liked the idea of the press but not the details of type and messy ink). I also needed a logo, so we looked to our heritage.

We considered one dynamic part of our distant past— the dramatic design of the Viking ship. As you may have noticed, we have brought Vikings to our present in several ways.

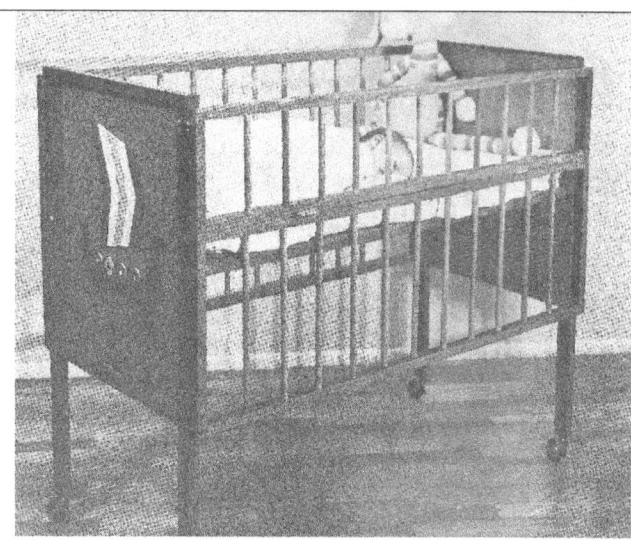

After all, they were literally part of our family's roots, because I even added cutouts of Viking ships to the crib I made for our kids (like a grade-school poster I created years before).

Once again, that crib "sailed" on to wider notice when *Sunset* magazine featured it in a story. Then, coincidentally, when *TIME* magazine ran a critical review of *Sunset*, *TIME* noted our crib.

Eventually, in this bit of family history, we no longer needed an infant's crib. But we liked the Viking design. So we re-purposed the end of the crib into a headboard for our guest bedroom.

But now—back to the drawing board for our printshop logo.

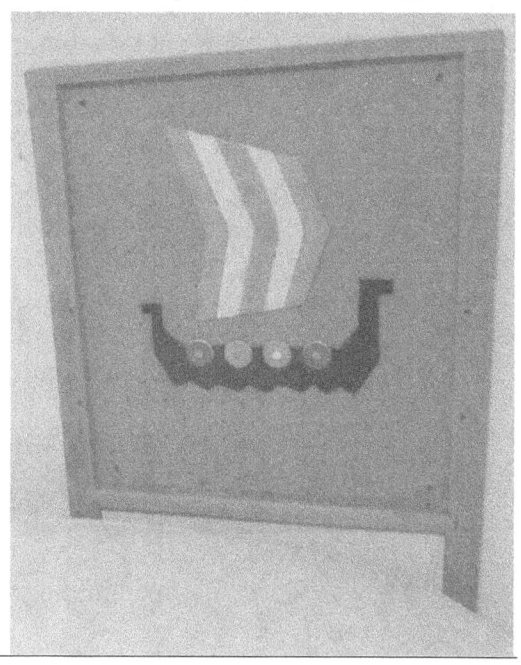

Then the familiar arrangement of Swedish crowns came to mind. Fits our Scandinavian "roots" and I could adapt but not steal the idea. So we came up with our "crown," or Krona in Swedish. Our "crown" prints well too. And our simple symbol adapts as shown here for the signs we wanted for our printshop.

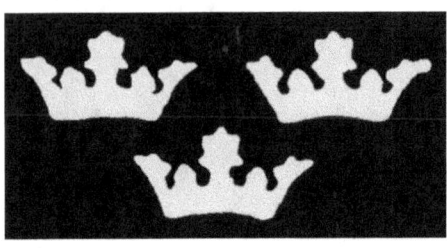
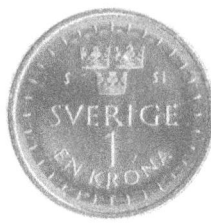

Plus, I could cut out our stylized crown design as shown below (again, like my third-grade cutting of the Scandinavian Billy Goat and the Troll).

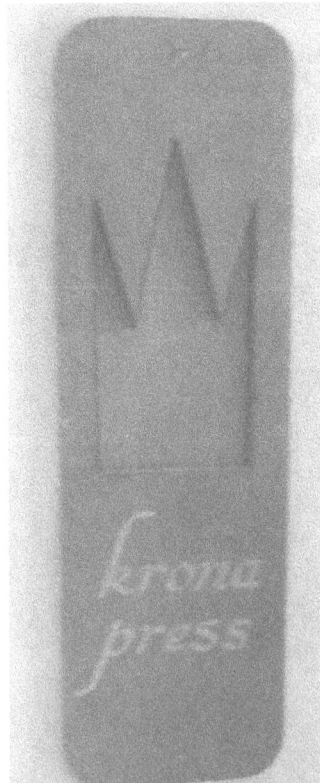

Unfortunately, the Baltic Blue of the metal behind this cutout sign doesn't show in this black-and-white printing.

Nor do the yellow words on the brown exterior hardboard.

Since then, I fastened that sign on the wall of our current office—above our present small Chandler & Price press.

Gradually, our family entered the naming game, as we analyzed and discussed and decided.

After all, we felt we should have a positive image for our small-scale operation, because we occasionally hosted some dignified visitors, not to mention the curious friends of our kids.

For instance, a college-professor friend would inquire every once in a while about dropping by for my show and tell—for students in his English class so they could get the feel for how written words turned into type for books.

When they arrived, our Krona Press signs greeted them, such as the weathered sign below that hung out for several years in the wet weather of Washington.

Now it too hangs with dignity near the small Chandler & Price press that serves as a decoration in our office. *To explain:* We do have a small press (6" x 9" platen) because our "big boy" weighed more than we wanted to move to California (more than a ton).

And we didn't have a pressroom that size anyway.

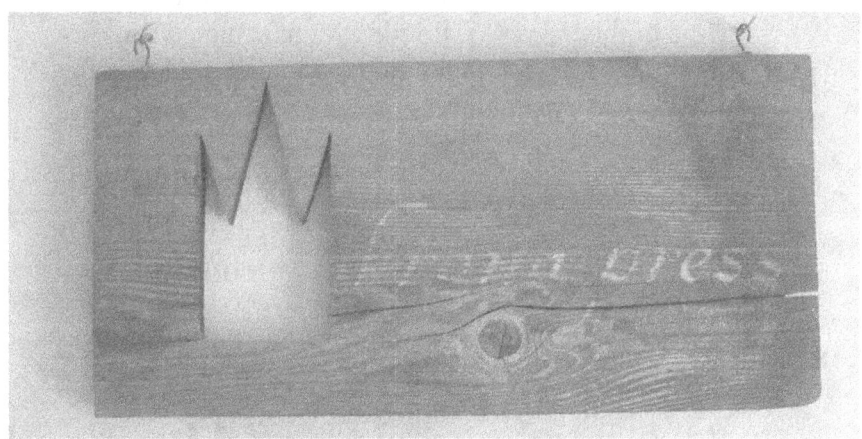

But we do appreciate this smaller press as a symbolic decoration in our office. And the signs to go with our mini-press (much less than a ton).

Maybe I'll even crank up that "baby" Chandler & Price some day.

As long as I don't mess up the room with ink and oil. But for now the press gets deluxe treatment in a carpeted room. Fortunately, we installed a plywood base to protect the carpet below.

Typically, this press now needs new composition rollers. But I learned about a local source when we visited the letterpress-training shop of Art Center College of Design in Pasadena.

At least I will feel safer with this small press. Just quit printing by pushing the lever up to avoid making an impression. No need for a brake to "stop the presses!" and halt all action of this press.

Meanwhile, I had at least learned to stay alert, keep my fingers out of harm's way, and maintain an even flow of paper in and paper out of the jaws of the big press.

But to grasp that…and much more…I had tracked down at our library info about an instruction book published by a printing instructor at Carnegie Tech.

So I ordered a text book directly from Prof. George J. Mills of the School of Printing Management. Thus, in the pre-Google era, that guide (and other books) helped me become a platen-press printer.

**So was this another correspondence course for me?**

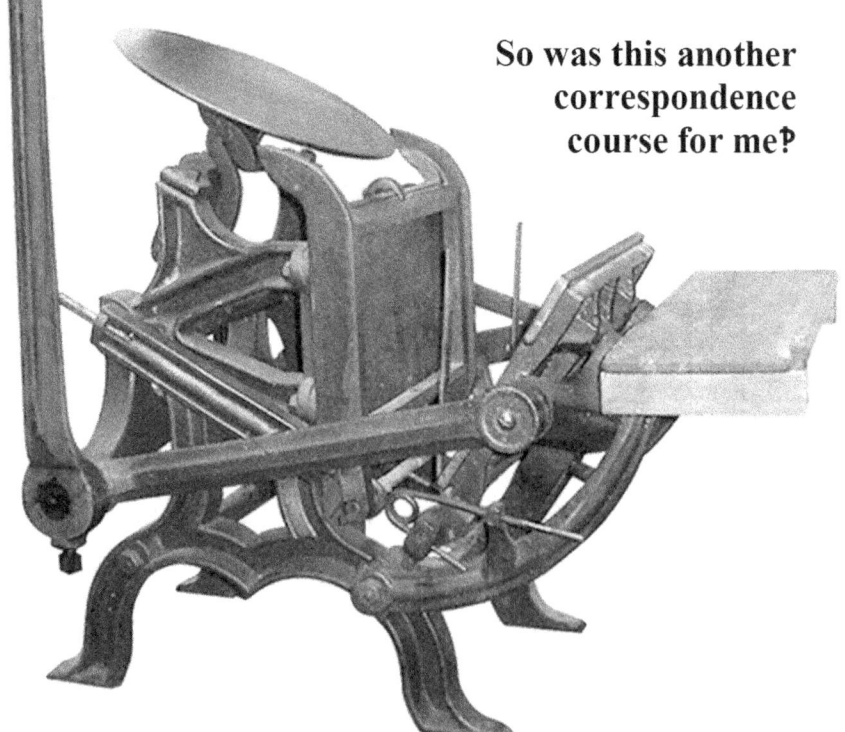

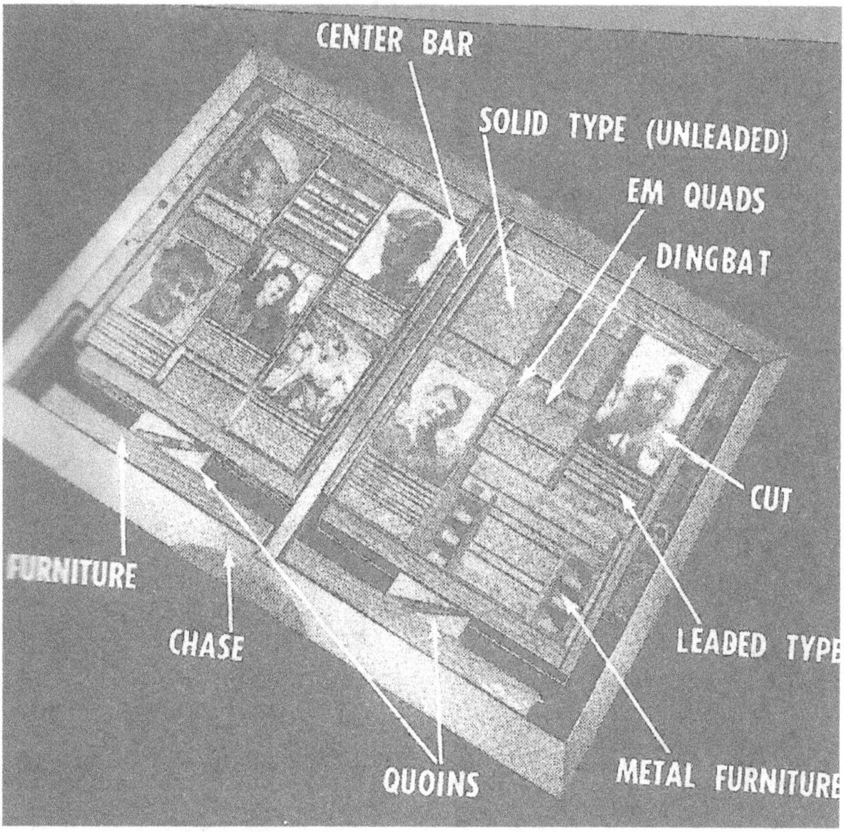

CENTER BAR

SOLID TYPE (UNLEADED)

EM QUADS

DINGBAT

CUT

FURNITURE

CHASE

LEADED TYPE

QUOINS

METAL FURNITURE

Meanwhile, the memories of setting up and locking a printing form have stayed with me.

When a form seems ready, prop up the form on a corner to push down and make sure some part doesn't slip...to "pi" the type.

Next, test again by imprinting a sheet on the press to be sure the type prints evenly. If not, back to the composing table to insert a brass spacer or put a piece of paper or tape under an offending letter.

So, all things considered, I think I'll stick with my computer, now that I've suffered through that learning curve too. Truthfully, still suffering, as changes seem to be continual.

Well, whether you're creating on the computer or setting type by hand or on the Linotype as shown at right, you do need to avoid confusion among letters, as noted on the cover of one of my novels.

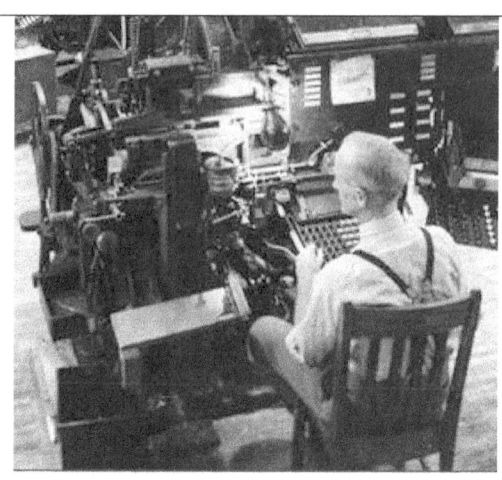

The risk: in hand-set type, the letters are backwards. So, beware!

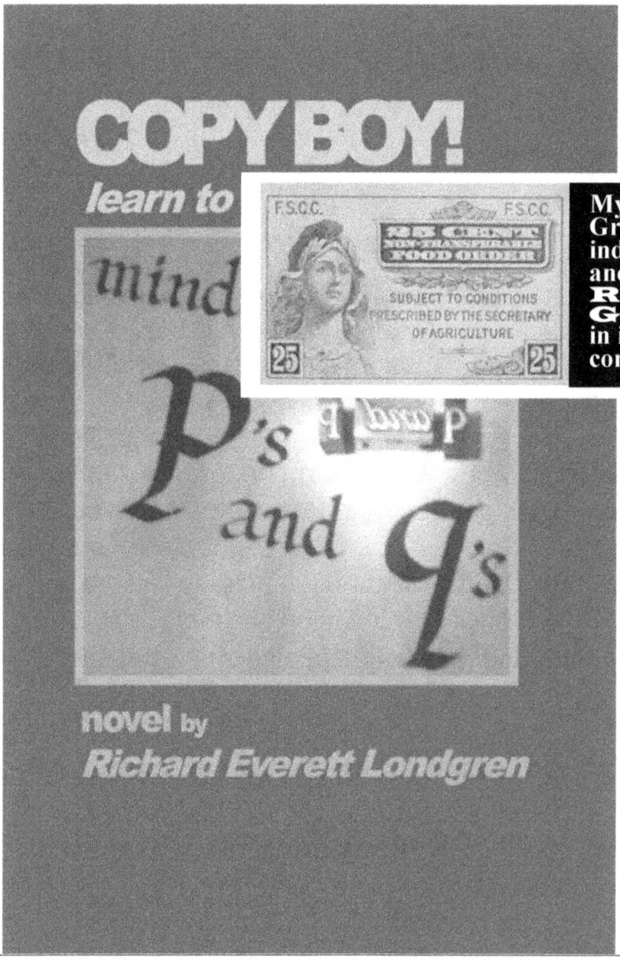

**COPY BOY!**

*learn to*

*mind*

*P's and q's*

*p's and p's*

My story set in the Great Depression indicates changing and expanding **RoleZ of the Government** in its evolving concern & control.

**novel** by

**Richard Everett Londgren**

## And mind your peeZ!

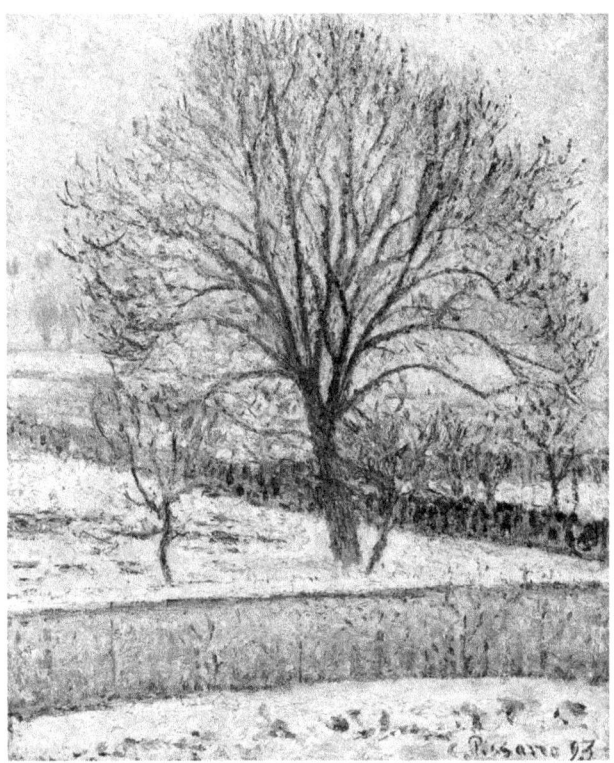

For us rural boys trudging through the snow, like in the bleak scene here, we left our mark when we stopped to "take a leak."

Don't just pee! For me, that offered another opportunity to create a design. Maybe the others just "drained," but I used that short burst to leave a monogram.

And, though we liked to eat snow when we got thristy, we learned from experience this warning— "never eat yellow snow!"

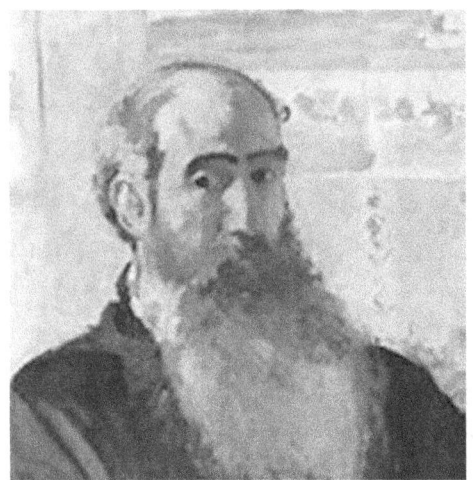

Years later, in writing my recollections about the Great Depression, I declared that my snow-art was inspired by the neo-impressionist Camille **Piss**aro. After all, he did paint that snow scene above, and I felt a link to his **Danish**-French ancestry.

And his name seemed appropriate.

## SignZ of changeZ

occurred slowly in the progress of printing—before the moveable type and Linotype evolved.

These woodcuts from my array of hand-crafted advertising blocks show the form used for earlier printing.

That sort of handwork evolved from China, on to Europe in the ninth Century, fostering a burgeoning paper and printing boom.

Eventually, artists such as Albrecht **Dürer** raised the level of design and craftsmanship.

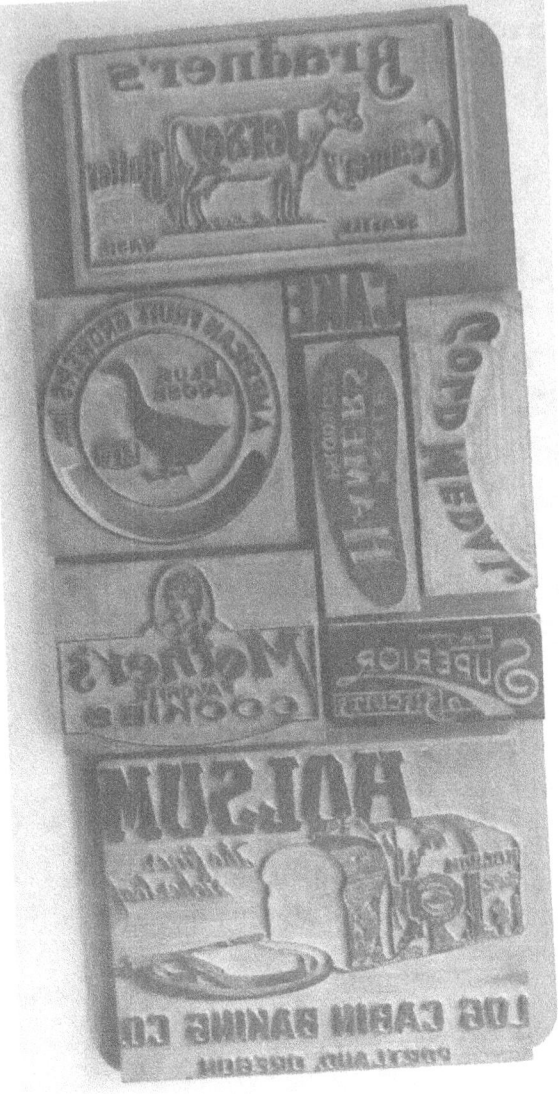

Engraving on end-grain blocks brought finer quality than the earlier plank-wise woodcuts.

Magazines in America, for instance, featured woodcuts and wood engravings before quality photo-reproduction evolved. More recently, noted artists have adopted and adapted the "relief block" for their expressions.

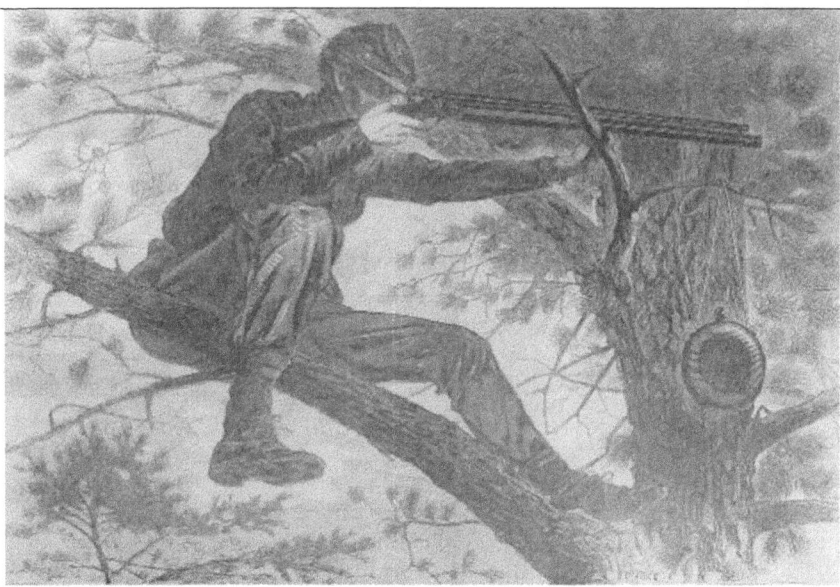

**Winslow Homer** captured my attention for several reasons, as this wood-block print helped illustrate the tragedy of the Civil War. And his scenes promoted my interest in history as a focus for me in college. Along with my concentration on English.

When our son Eric was a toddler, I used to carry him around and point out scenes to him from our collection of Winslow Homer prints. As a result, Eric's first word was "duck"—inspired by a Winslow Homer print.

We obtained those prints from the National Gallery of Art. To allow for a "changing of the gu*arf*" occasionally, I created special frames that facilitated the sliding of those standard-size prints in from the top.

So those prints from the Gallery not only enriched our "gallery," they nudged my imagination in creating the "re-purposing" frames.

Like some of my other ideas, the frames caught the attention of *Sunset* nagazine.

So the concept of a frame…and the prints…got wider attention.

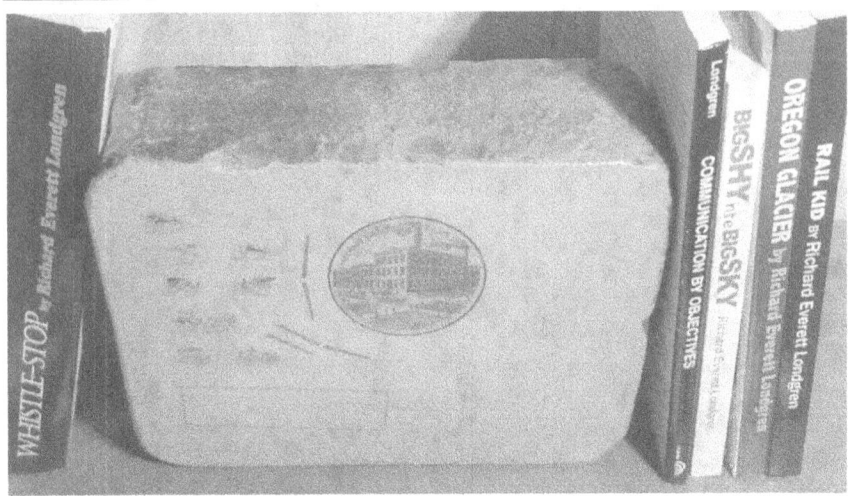

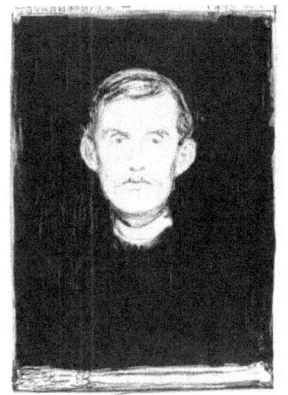

In my Krona Press collection, this **lithography** limestone printing block not only decorates, it reminds me that Norwegian artist **Edvard Munch** created his self-portrait at left on such a block. And he carved this woodcut version below of his famous **The Scream**. And three noted Norwegians came together in a special poster: Designed by **Munch,** it included writer **Henrik Ibsen** and composer **Edvard Grieg**.

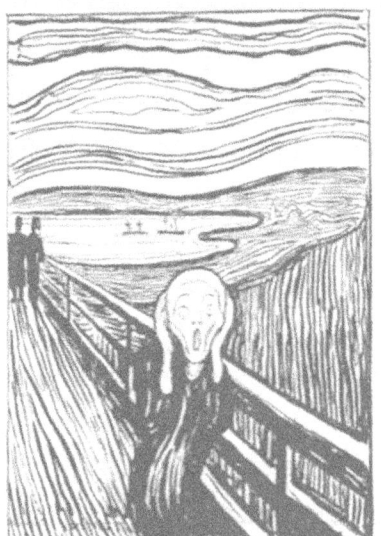

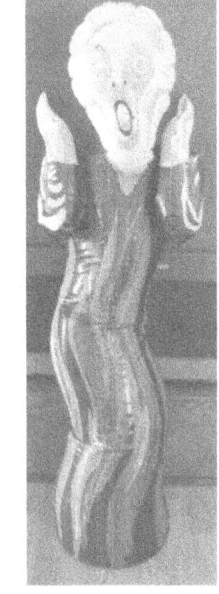

And at our Scandinavian Center, visitors enjoy seeing this inflatable version of his painting of **The Scream**.

## More ado about Leonardo!

In my *Whistle-Stop* novel, **da Vinci's** "dimensions of man" provides an interesting reaction in a high school class.

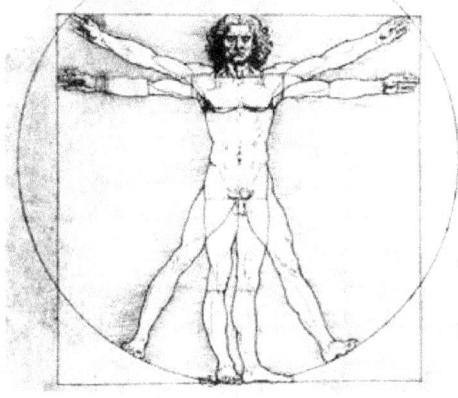

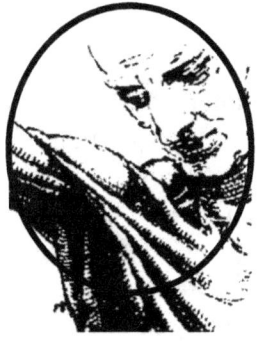

His detailed drawings relate to my earlier reference about "air-brushed anatomy."

And, in this book, I also mentioned his "mirror writing." Beyond me, I admit.

Of course, his painting of the "Last Supper" probably ranks as his most memorable accomplishment.

His artistic achievements certainly impressed me, but I can't say that he inspired me—because his talent as a giant in art far exceeded my aspirations.

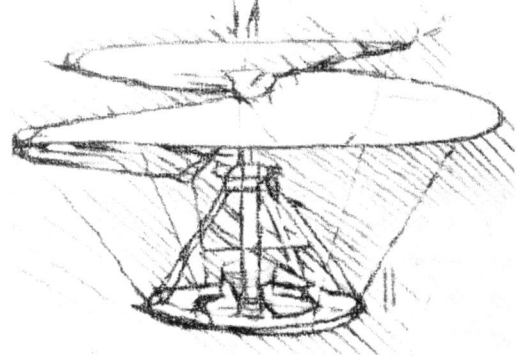

But da Vinci's inventions did impress and inspire me as they showed the scope of his imagination.

He seemed to be always ready to invent whatever might fit a need.

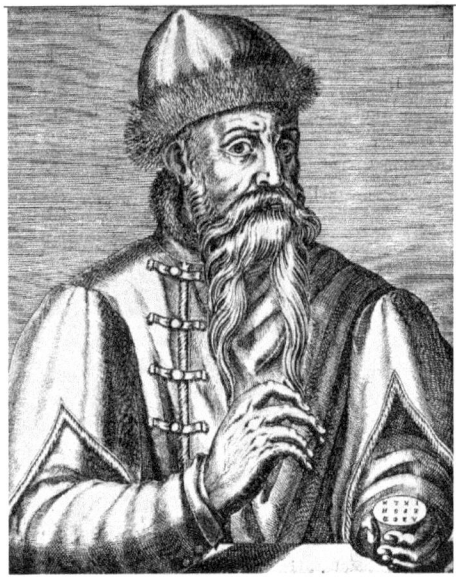

Leonardo even conceived some improvements in the printing press of his time. Alas, he didn't get a request to develop moveable type, so that invention had to wait a few more years.

And years later, someone else did come up with the concept of moveable type—when **Johannes Gutenberg** caused a virtual revolution in communication with that advancement…not long after da Vinci and the Middle Ages.

Then, centuries later, **Ottmar Mergenthaler** contributed to another advancement in printing by creating his complicated Linotype machine, while **Mark Twain** had spent a fortune in vain on a more-complicated type-setting machine.

About that time, **Thomas Edison** and his team provided "on-demand" communication inventions, including the phonograph and movies.

And printing too, with the Mimeograph.

Now, the computer and Internet offer vast horizons of communication—that bogle the mind of this kid from rural Minnesota.

So, maybe I'll just offer a simple "Thank You!" to all of those inventors…and hold my breath for what might come next!

# But is it art?

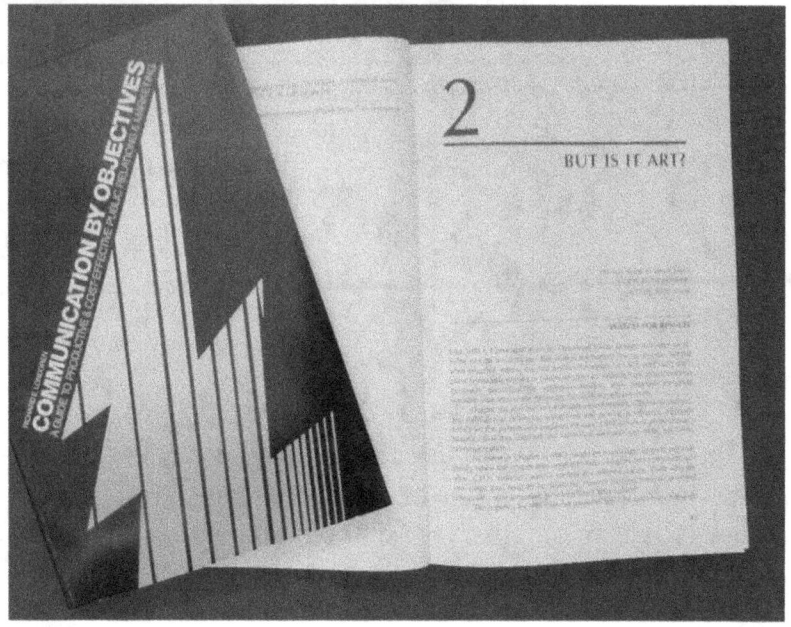

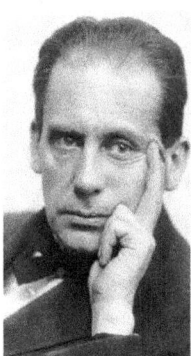

**Walter Gropius**

In my communication book shown here, that's the kind of question founder **Walter Gropius** of Bauhaus in Germany raised as he related art to architecture, publishing and other practical applications of fresh-thinking about communication.

And, as a former elementary school teacher, **Josef Albers** taught the Bauhaus students to get back to the basics of design by cutting and pasting and folding—a primitive form like I practiced with my Billy Goat Gruff cutting early on.

Not exactly **origami** and **kirigami**, but challenging as simple art forms.

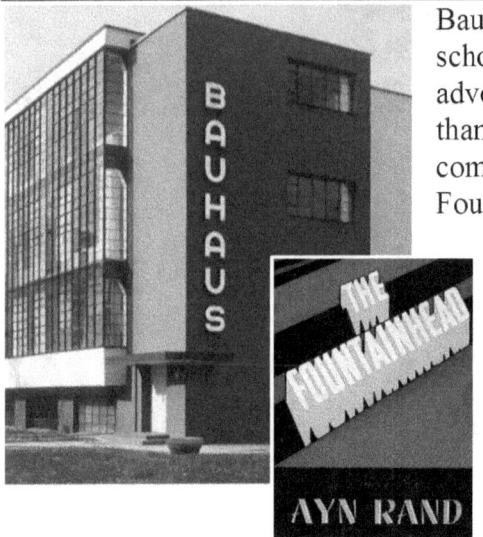

Bauhaus, the counter-culture school of the '30s, served as an advocate of pragmatic rather than emotion-driven design and communication.

Founder **Walter Gropius** declared his independence from romanticizing hand crafting while advocating the application of the machine to industry and to modern life.

In her novel *THE FOUNTAINHEAD*, **Ayn Rand** offers a parallel theme of a defiant architect reacting to **changeZ** of purposes, possibilities and desires, as well as capitalizing on evolving materials and capabilities.

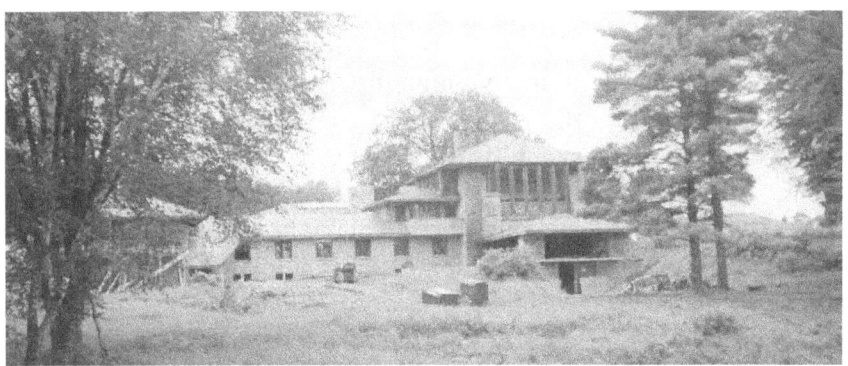

**Frank Lloyd Wright** also sought new methods and materials in architecture and explored new concepts, especially in his later designs. Yet, he also strived to link the future with the past.

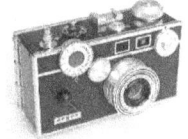

**View of Frank Lloyd Wright's Taliesin in Wisconsin taken by me with my Argus C3 in 1953.**

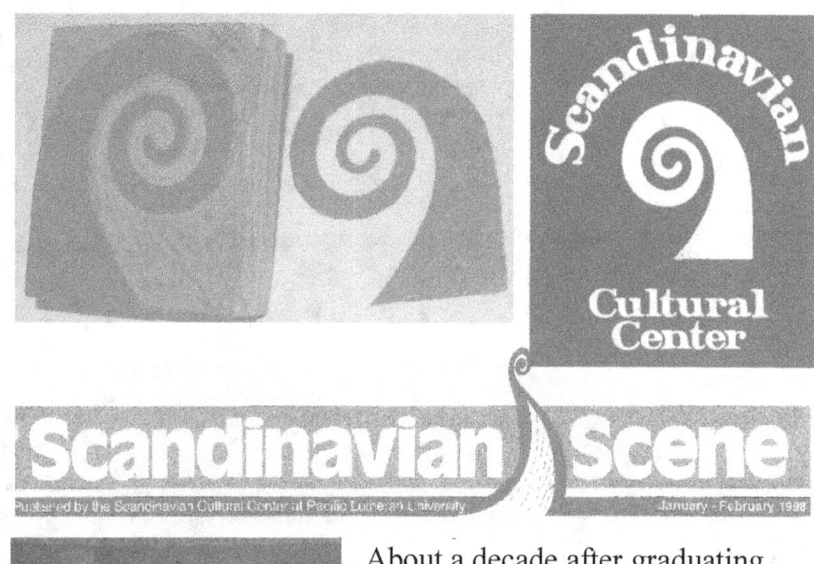

Scandinavian Cultural Center

**Scandinavian Scene**

Published by the Scandinavian Cultural Center at Pacific Lutheran University          January - February, 1998

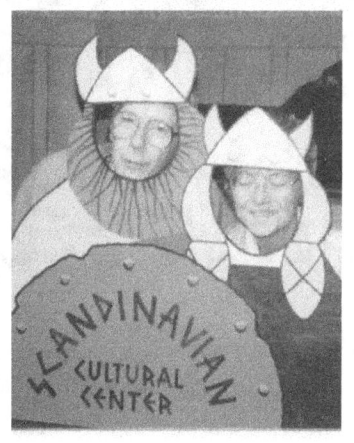

About a decade after graduating from Pacific Lutheran College, my wife and I began to get involved in the alumni organization and attending an occasional event.

Then the new **Scandinavian Cultural Center** opened in the Student Union building, and we got a call to "get on board"—as on a Viking ship⸮

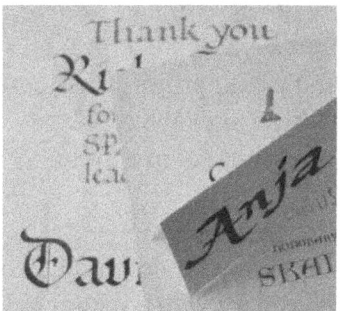

Before long, I became writer, photographer and editor of the newsletter. And creating the "photo op" cutout display Anita and I are peeking through, and producing the special forms as shown at left. And I eventually became president for a term. Then we moved to California.

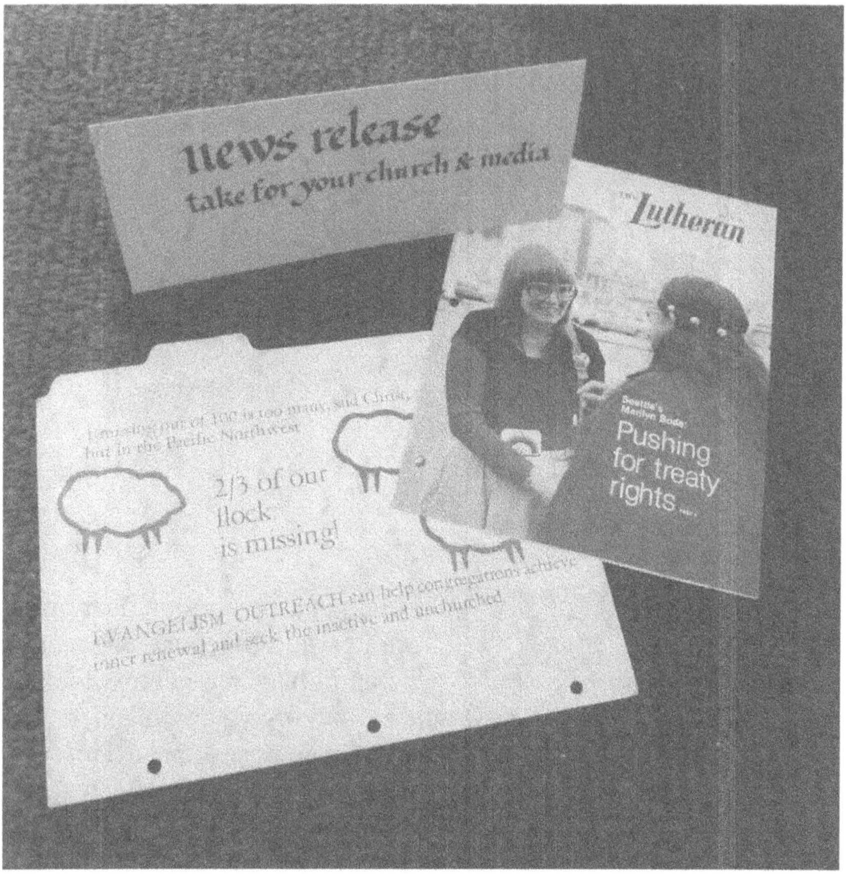

Meanwhile, my Journalism Professor (also a Pastor) at Pacific Lutheran had enlisted me as a volunteer communicator for the regional and national Lutheran Church. That also involved writing, photography and design as indicated by the assemblage above.

My antique platen press participated, including printing the text and my Linoleum-cut blocks of sheep "bleating" about the evangelism theme on a file folder for a regional convention.

Eventually, a regional Lutheran assembly honored me with a Bishop's Award to cap my 30 years as a volunteer communicator, which included serving eight years with others on the nationwide Lutheran communication committee.

# SignZ at Home

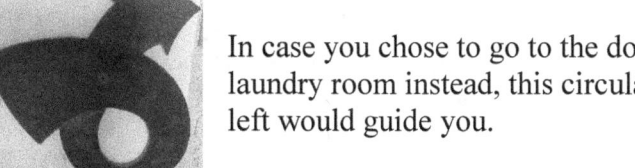

In our four-story house in Tacoma, we found signs to be useful in more places than our detached garage with our Krona Press.

If you took the back stairway to the second floor, you might get a lesson about the alphabet.

Just hold on the hand-rail as you ascend (or descend) while noting the series of posters with individual letters and a brief history of each. Just don't trip as you trip through the alphabet!

Below, note the sign for directions as you go down to the basement to shoot pool or play Ping-Pong, where you'd find an array of other signs.

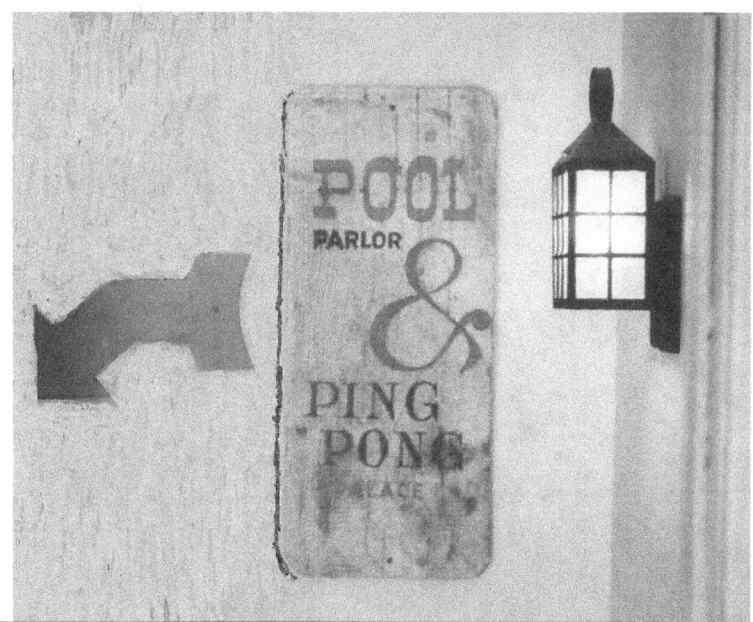

In case you chose to go to the downstairs laundry room instead, this circular sign at left would guide you.

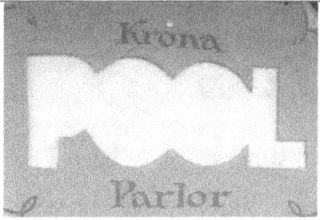

I cut out this pool sign to be lighted from behind, to call attention to our "Pool Parlor and Ping-Pong Palace" in our basement. Then I lettered the name and rules for pool on the underside of the Ping-Pong table to hang on the wall…as shown with our three kids at a game of pool. When we moved away from our "poolhall" we hung the table as a decoration along the fence in California.

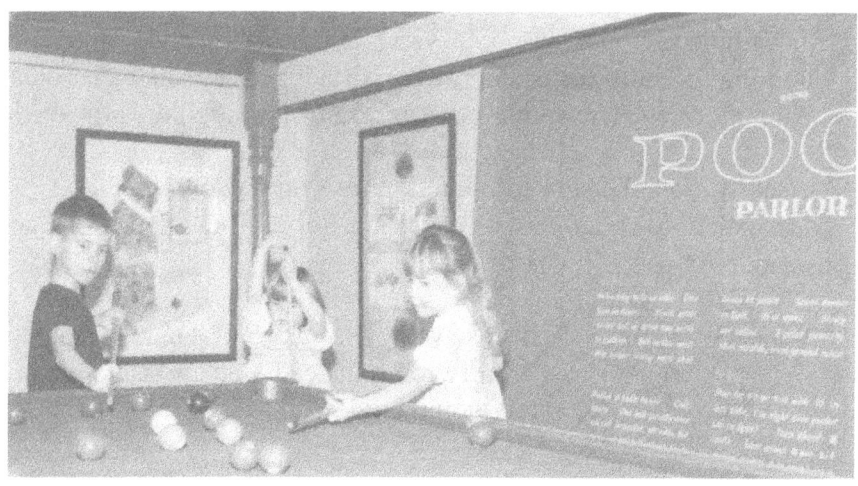

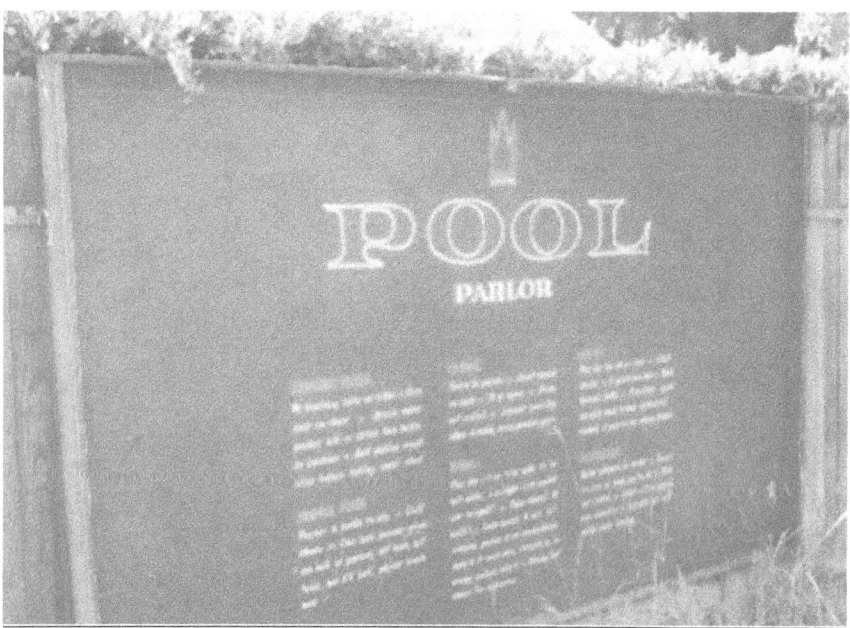

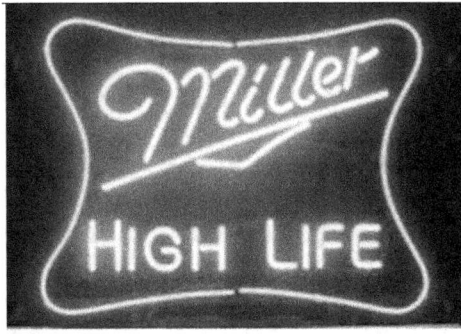

Another conspicuous form of our 20th Century communication cast a warm glow in our "pool parlor"—a neon light promoting beer.

But definitely no service to minors, though!

On the street, a related glowing enticement also got attention from our kids—the "appetizing" lighted "pizza" sign atop a delivery car.

Meanwhile, the kids from school and our neighborhood turned their attention to our antique candy machine—which we kept stocked with bargains for the kids. Today's candy at yesterday's prices!

Believe me, those kids knew a "sweet" bargain when they saw one.

So the "machine age" had arrived in our basement, and we occasionally had to put a lid on it. Or go broke from "loss leaders."

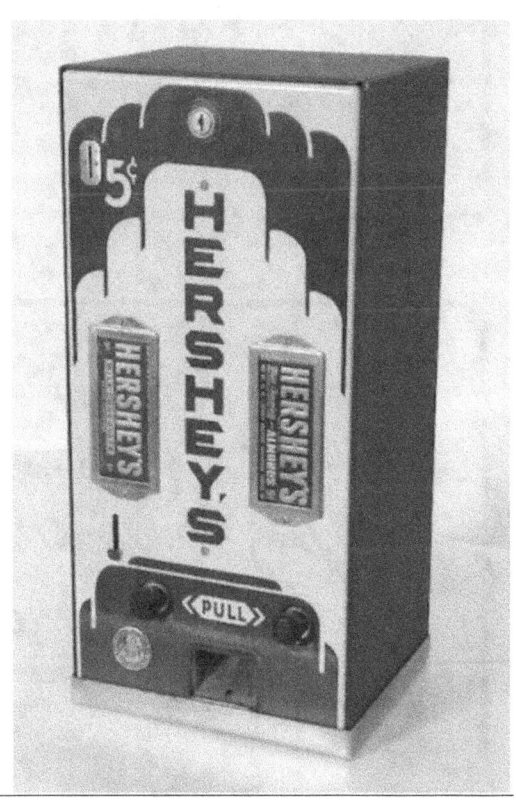

Reminds me of the envy my brother and I experienced with a one-cent Hershey bar we brought for our Country School lunch from our *Country Store*. (See pages 5, 19 &141 for my story of school & store.)

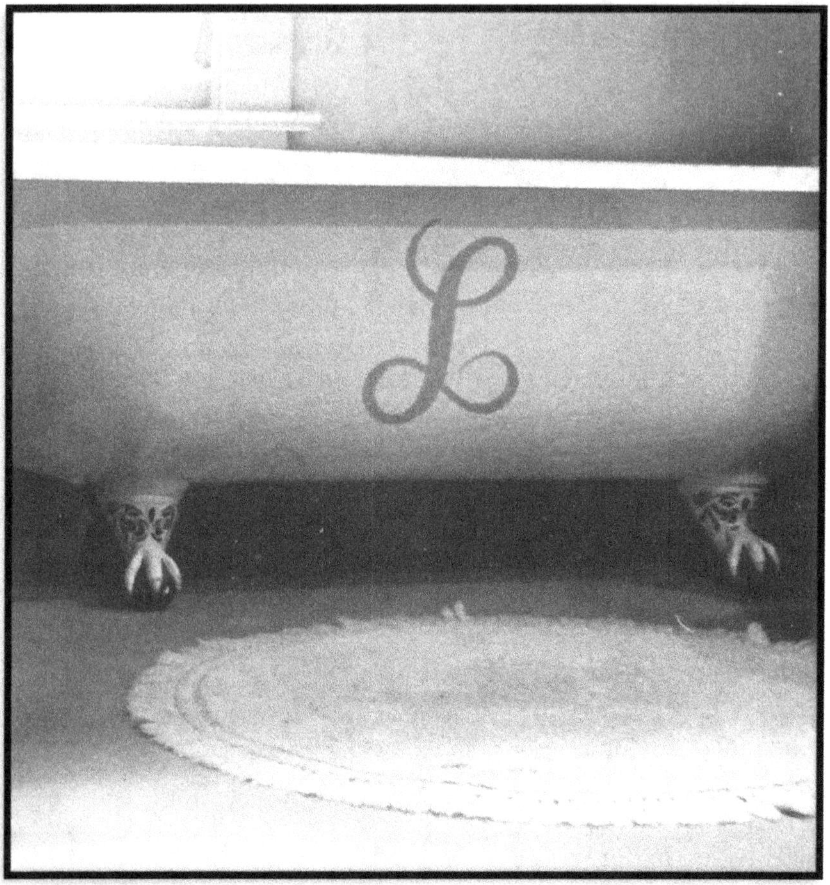

*Even our claw-foot bathtub seemed to want special attention…so I added our monogram.*

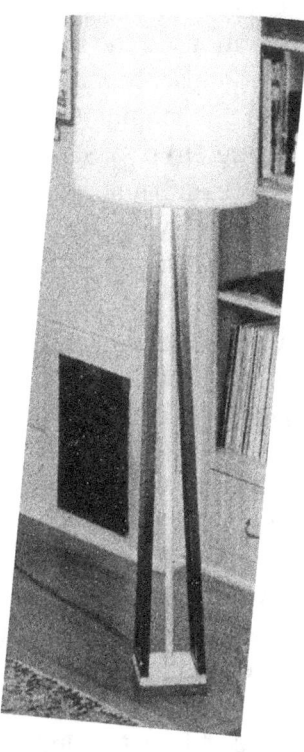

This lamp looks a bit tipsy in our living room, even though I loaded the base with un-reusable lead Linotype slugs. (Well, the lamp did take some spills despite "weighty" words.)

The more-stable lamps on end-tables got type too—obviously meant to support reading lamps.

So, the special lead weights certainly show the importance of words set into type!

P.S. The wood uprights demonstrate geometry, like calligraphy, with joinery angles of 30 degrees.

The legs of some tables pictured later also depended on calligraphy—45-degree angles for pens set the angle of cuts to stabilize the legs.

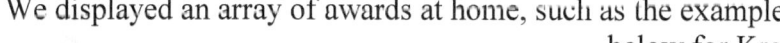

We displayed an array of awards at home, such as the example

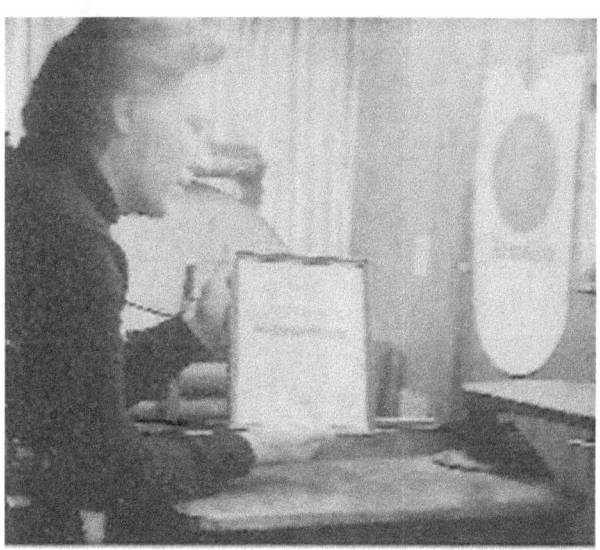

below for Krona Press. But note that Ben Franklin in poster at right watches to verify appropriateness of the printing honor.

Meanwhile, I helped design and arrange for laser-cut wood plaques for Weyerhaeuser retirees. Like me.

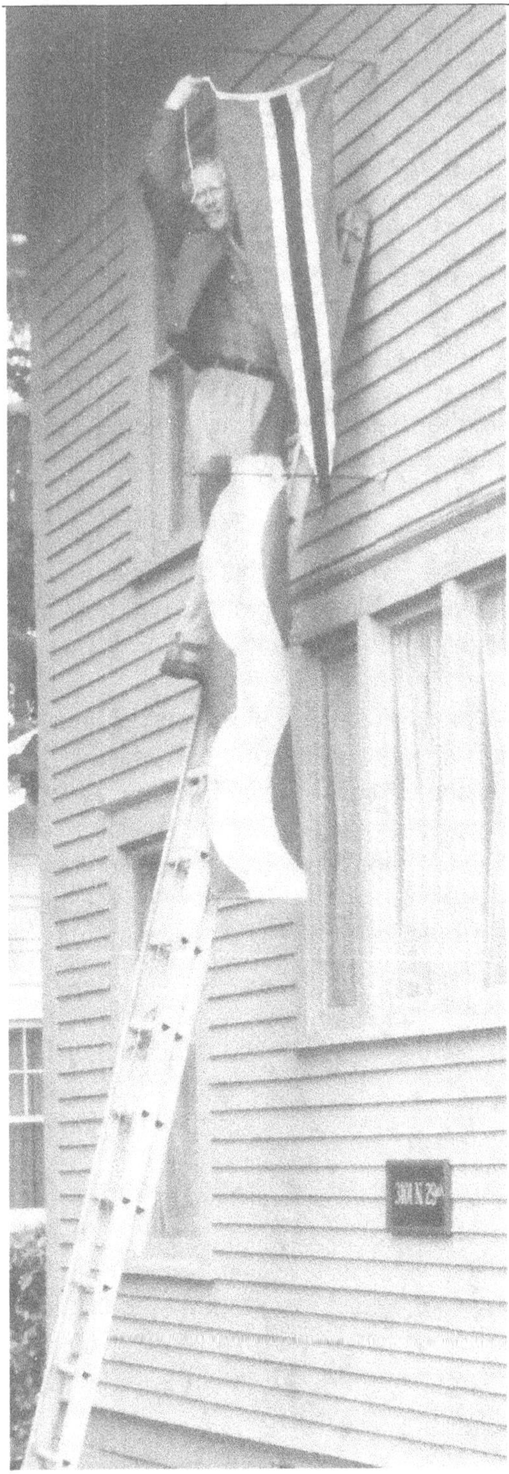

We didn't limit the decorations to the inside of our house, because here I am hanging (and hanging on) a Norwegian banner high above the Swedish design already in place.

When a large outside porch floor needed repainting, we decided to just paint a design on the worn areas with waves related to our view of Puget Sound. And for the worn hallway floor in the basement, we painted a blue whale—also tied to waters of Puget Sound.

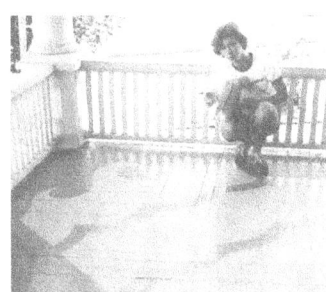

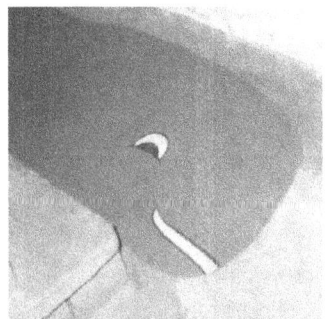

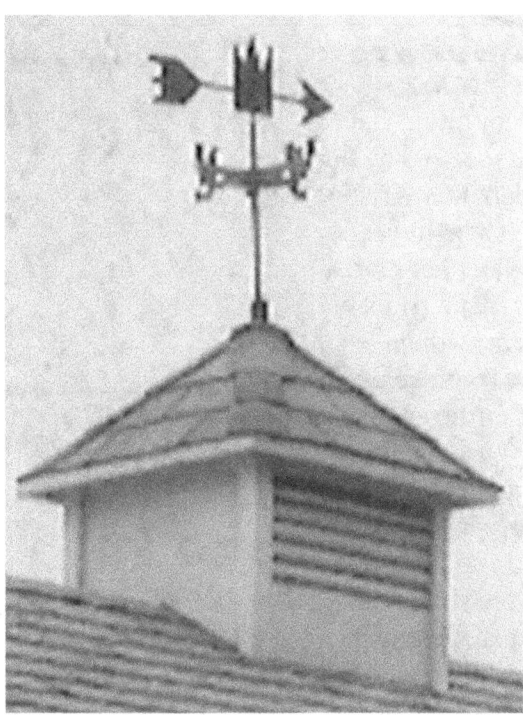

Our garage and printshop needed decoration and ventilation, so we added this cupola. (Note the crown.) And our kids liked to climb up and in—where they could shout down to the alley at their friends—and startle any innocent passersby. They could watch the neighborhood basketball "hoop shoot." That may have inspired a benefit game (below) set up later by our daughter Karin.

# H⬤⬤PS
# for Health
*Celebrity
Basketball
Benefit*

**Londgren Logs**

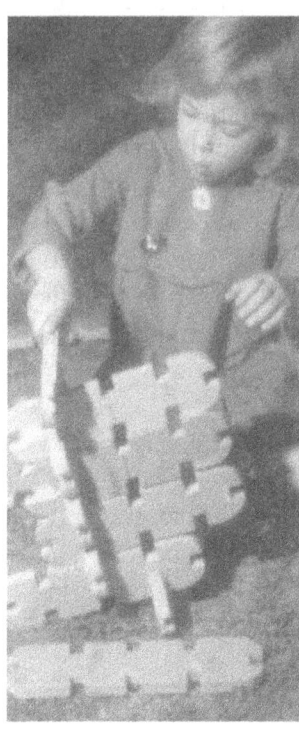

got tested (left) in the '70s by our daughter Kristin. Then 40 years later her niece Anja (right) stacks them also. To make our **Londgren Logs**, I used cutouts (again!) from the marine plywood I used to make the slide in my patent-drawing shown below (note the calligraphy too).

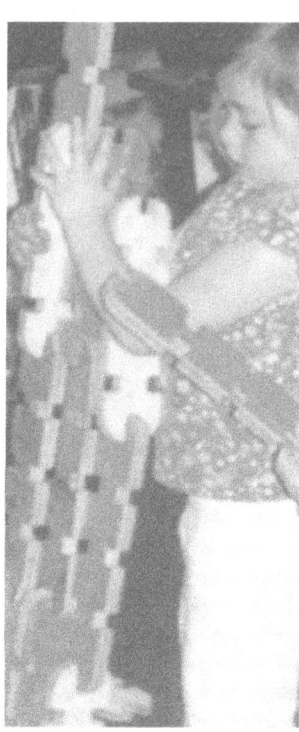

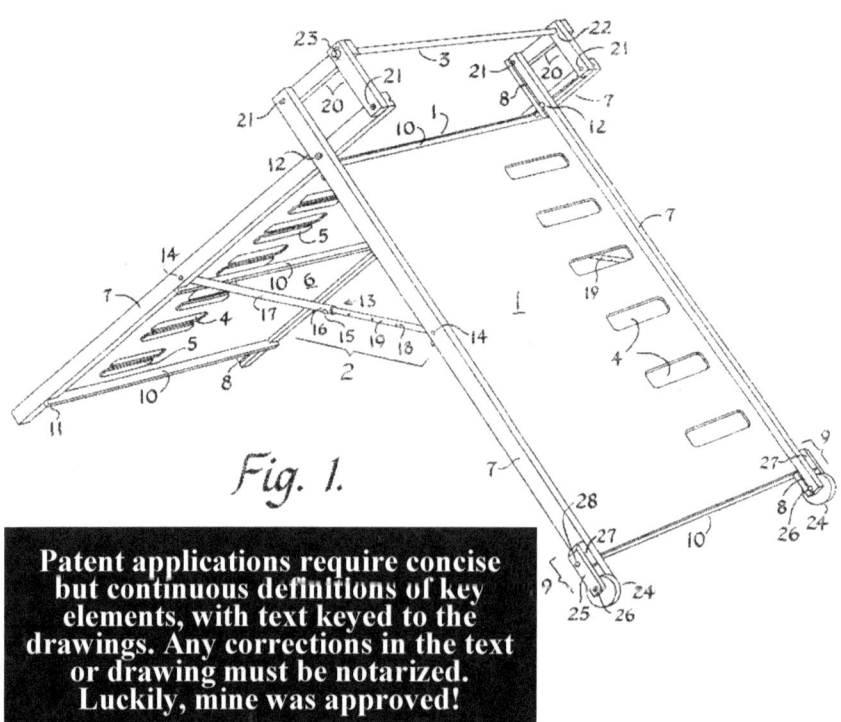

*Fig. 1.*

Patent applications require concise but continuous definitions of key elements, with text keyed to the drawings. Any corrections in the text or drawing must be notarized. Luckily, mine was approved!

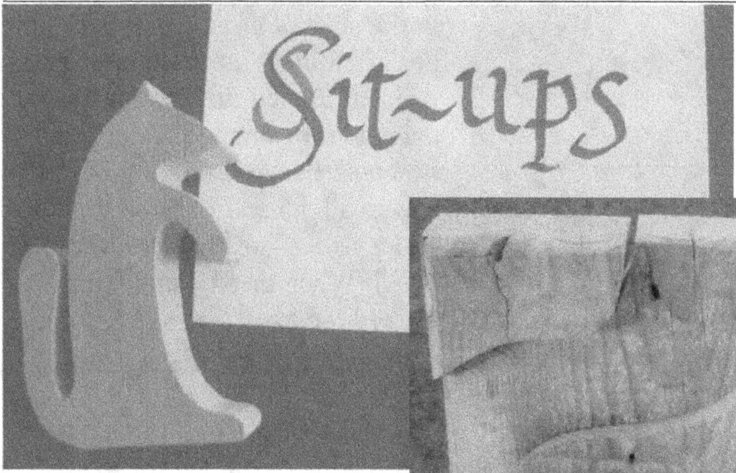

# $\mathcal{S}$it~ups

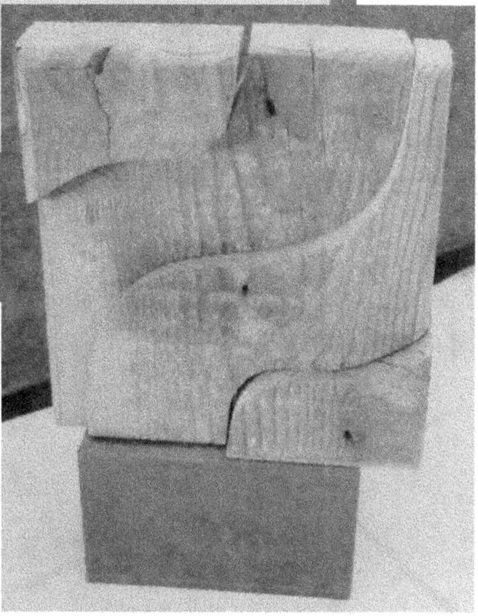

When creating cutouts in the past, I featured the Billy Goat, of course, and pigs…even a duck. When I broke coping-saw blades to shape a pig as a breadboard, my Dad urged me to "keep on coping." I did.

But I used my bandsaw to shape the gopher above as a reminder to stick with my exercise regimen. Ironically, the University of Minnesota "championed" the Gopher as a mascot…but the state paid us kids a "bounty" to eliminate the gophers from the land.

Meanwhile, with the bandsaw ready for further action, I cut (and sanded) the scrap block above into my favorite abstract sculpture.

For the gopher, I invoked calligraphy to help promote a message. And, once again, I took some liberties with the forms…of the gopher and the calligraphy.

In a short application such as this, I could "go back to the drawing board!" if I made a mistake to simply "start over!" However, in calligraphing long documents, starting over may not be an option. Thus, the unofficial protocal of calligraphy allows "careting" a space and adding small letters or words of correction above the line of lettering.

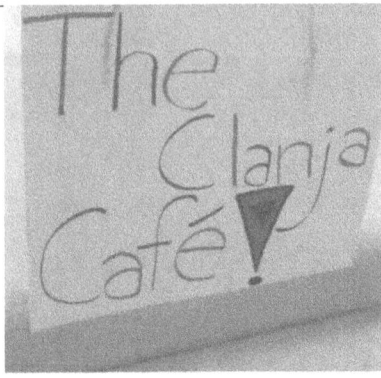

In the spirt of artistic expression, our grand-daughters Claire and Anja combined their names ◄ for the café they created at our house. Much earlier, when their Dad Eric was a kid, he and I "slobbered" paints as an "abstract" on a wood panel. When dried, I cut and framed the "best" part… and it still decorates our living room.

In another throwback, if Claire and Anja needed café furnishings, they could revert to small tables ▼ I made and named for their Dad and aunts Kristin and Karin. Those individualized tables continue to be sturdy 40 years later.

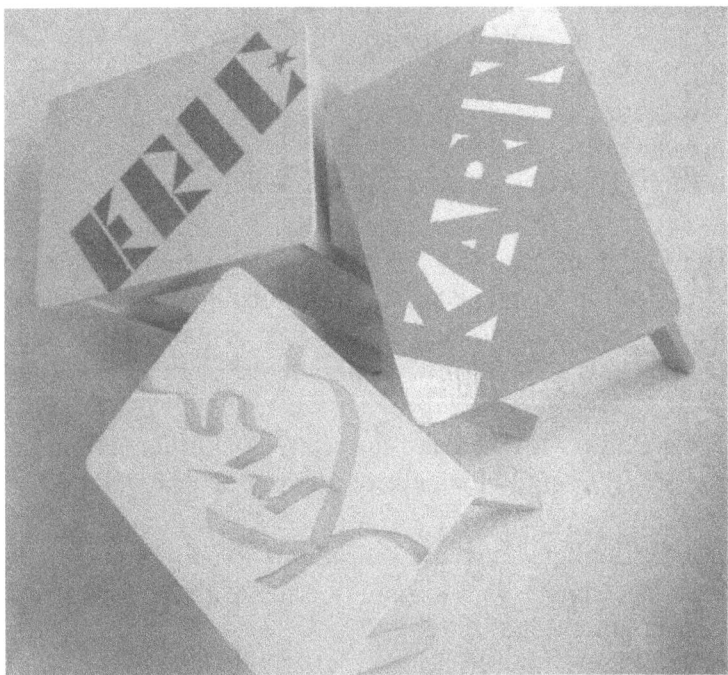

Remember, as shown here, in case of a paint spill that can't be removed, sign-painting can come in handy to just admit the mistake.

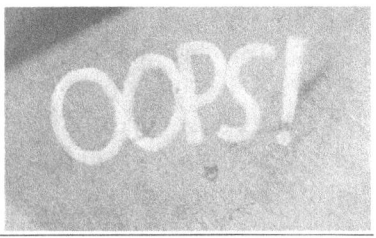

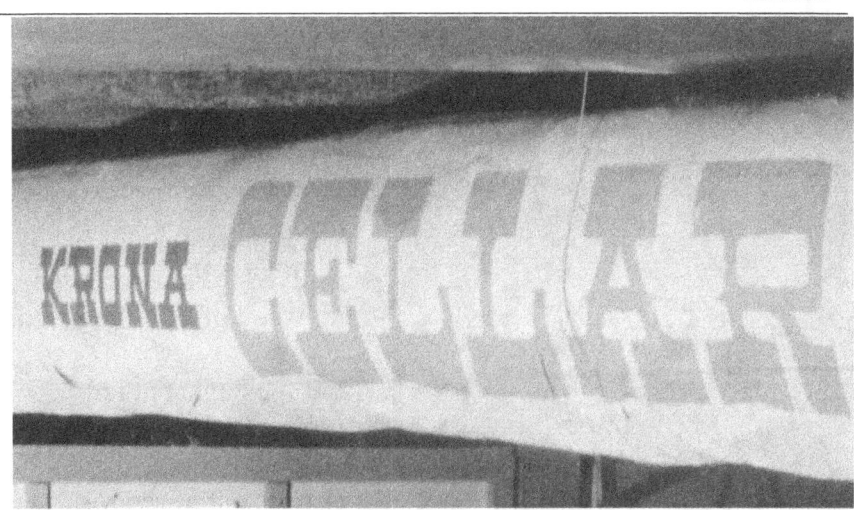

Some of our signs decorated and even "camouflaged" our basement, such as the lettering on a furnace pipe and the super-graphics at right.

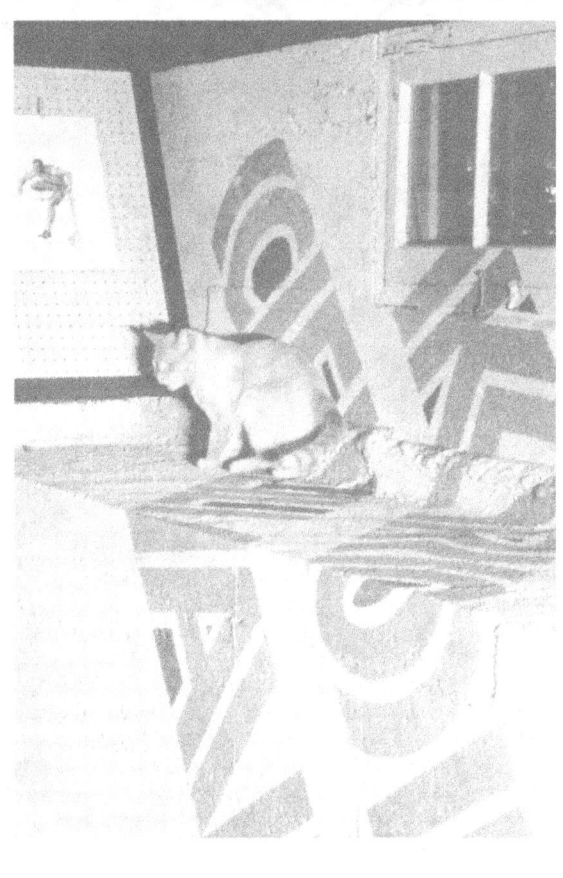

Below, I'm adding "up" to the warning about the ledge at different floor levels.

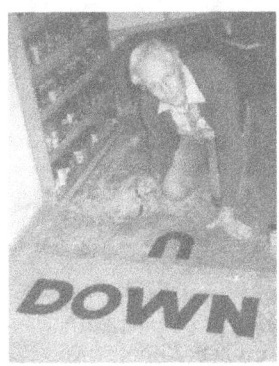

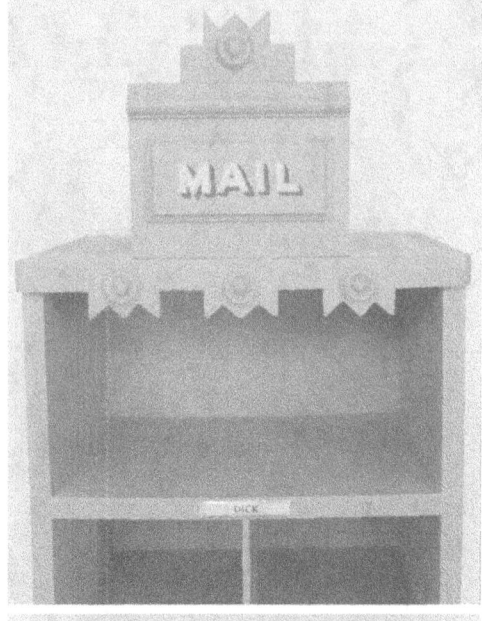

Our Nordic designs here show a new/old look, with the "salvaged crowns" on our family mailbox.

Another mailbox also evolved from repurposed plywood of a parking sign.

For the banner at left below, I set up an "assembly line" to cut the crosses out of scrap hardboard. Then I painted the crosses blue and yellow and glued them on a remnant of brown upholstery fabric.

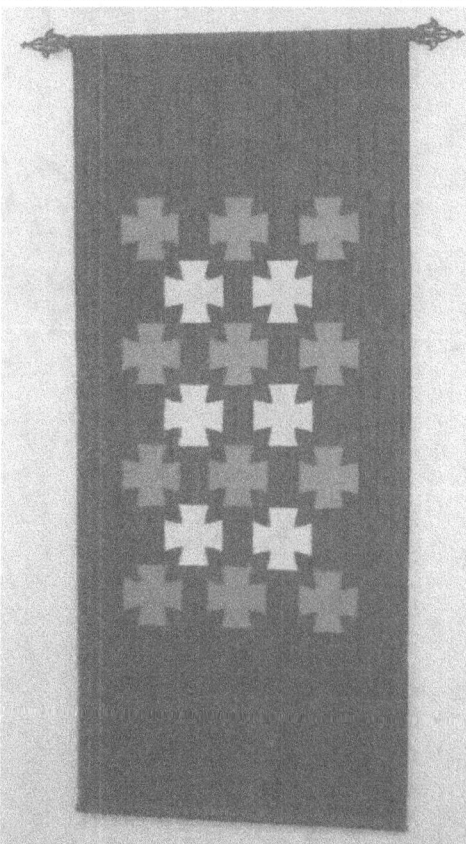

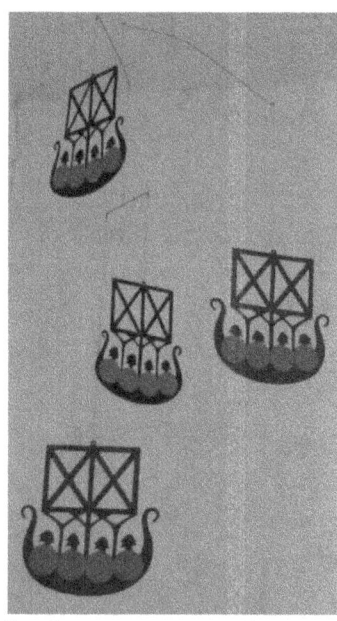

In the same room, these floating cutout Viking ships "sail"—suspended from the ceiling.

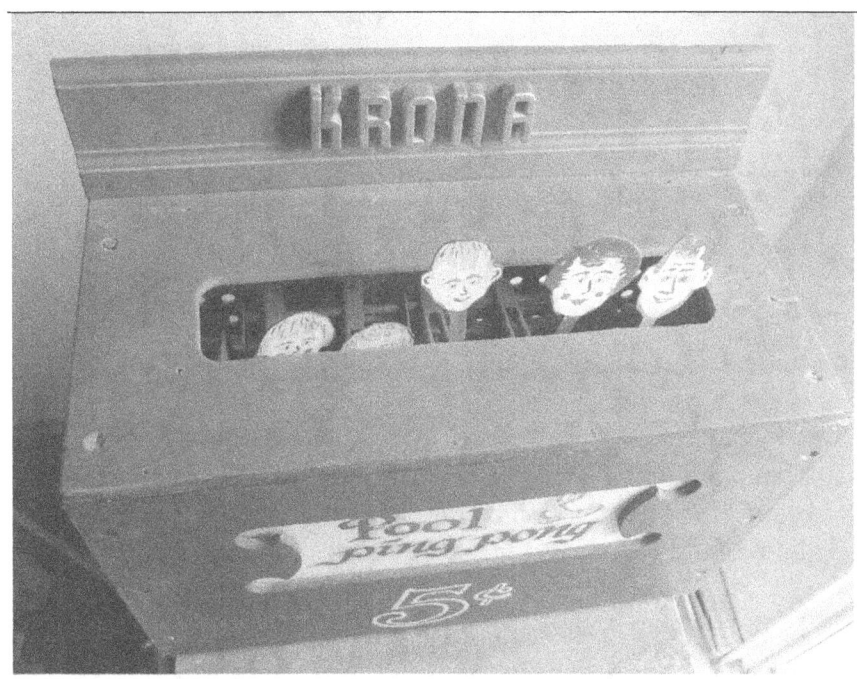

As an introduction to our family, I created this mechanized, lighted family portrait. The heads pop up and down, but I couldn't get them all up at the same time for the photo. Symbolic?

After I improvised the film editor below, I had to add our "Krona" name, of course, to give it a "look" like Hollywood.

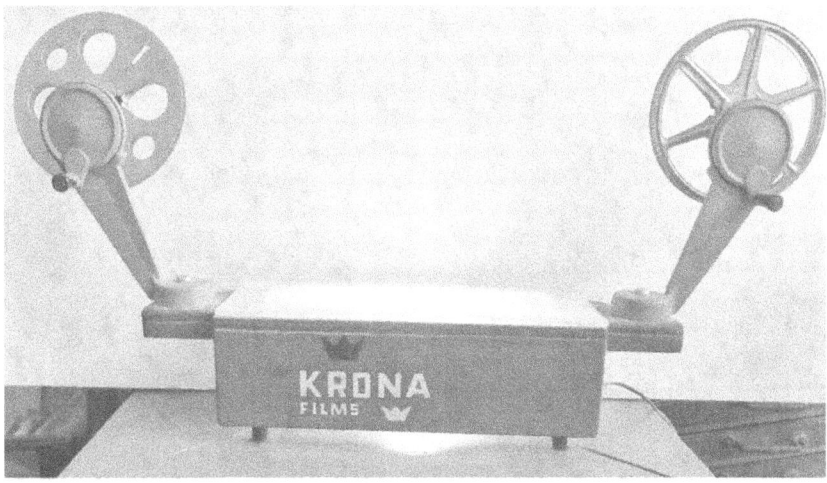

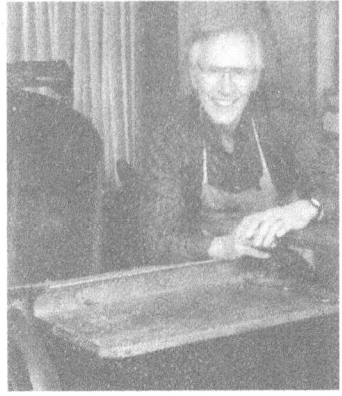
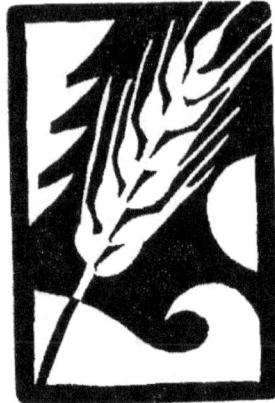

Here I am in our Krona Press printshop, where I carved and printed the logo for Anita's family history above. Below, the grain design I carved and printed indicates my rural background.

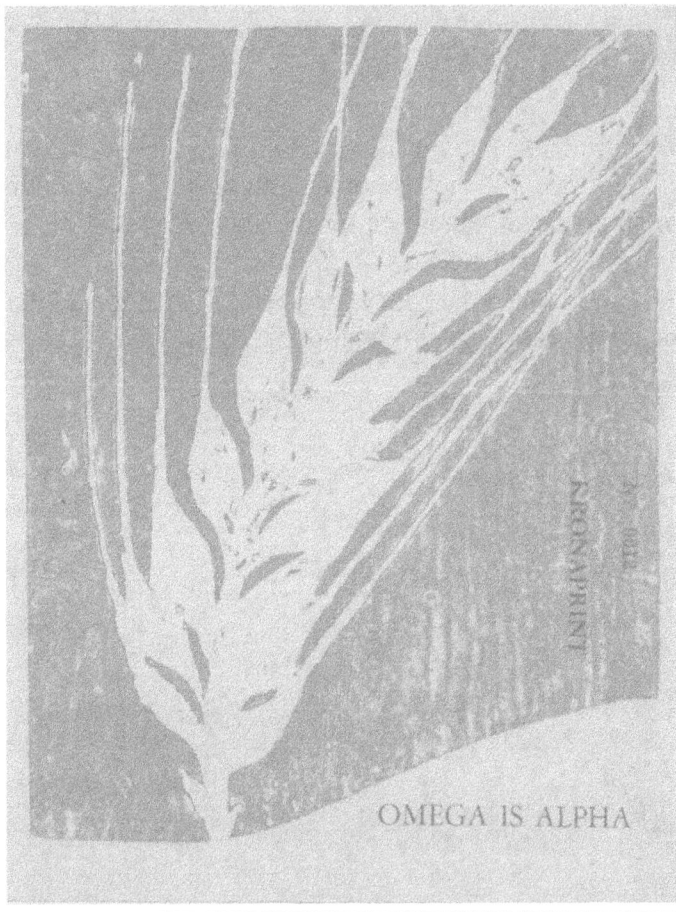

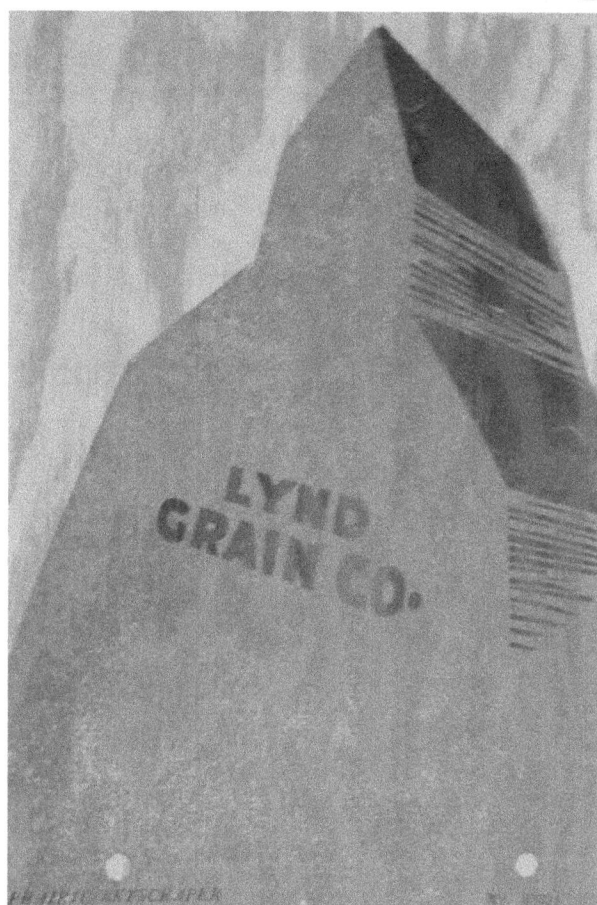

To promote the **SignZ and SoundZ**, I printed this poster *Prairie Skyscraper* about the grain elevator across the highway from our gas station/house. Trains rumbled in to get that stored grain. For us bare-foot kids, the tracks offered a short-cut to swim at **Camden** State **Park**. We could "ruff-it" on cinders and hot ties and rails of Great Northern or go easier-on-the-feet but longer by the road.

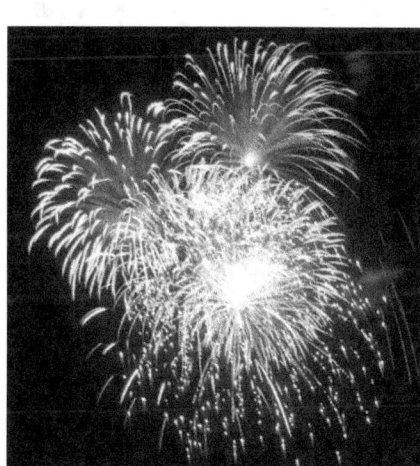

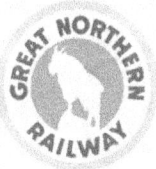

Each summer, Lyndwood's Fourth of July celebration offered the dazzling fireworks display from a bluff high above the Great Northern tracks.

Years later, we could see from our Tacoma house the fireworks set off from a barge towed by a tugboat out into Commencement Bay.

Evidently deer could read the sign on the "**grain**" elevator, because when I set out early in the morning to deliver the newspapers, I might see a herd of them gathered to mooch spilled grain for their daily breakfast.

Of course, Minnesota posted warning signs about deer and other wildlife as a highway threat to motorists. As if the blizzards weren't enough to worry about!

In Sweden, my relatives reported that signs warning about moose crossing the roads disappeared as collectibles for tourists.

So Swedish entrepreneurs offered low-cost imitation signs as memorabilia. That satisfied the tourists and saved the warnings for drivers. Well, Swedes and Volvos believe in safety on the road. Don't know about tourists!

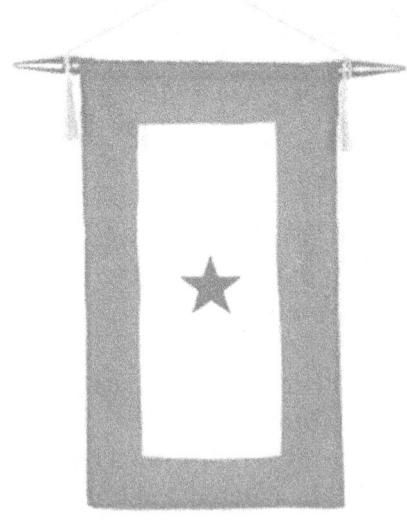

Sadly, while I delivered papers during World War II, I repeatedly felt the shock of war headlines. Then, along my route, I got personal reminders of the war as I passed signs like this—displayed in windows of homes with a person in military service.

Later, as a grim reminder, I saw at least two homes with a special sign indicating a person from that family had been killed in action some time during the 1940s.

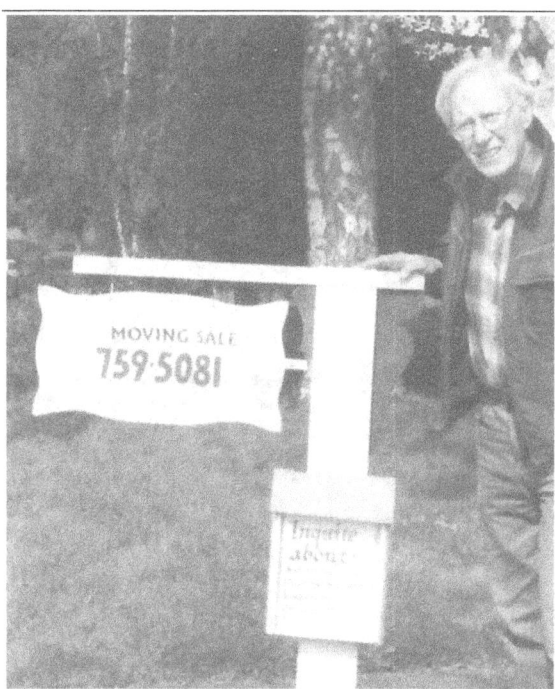

When we faced downsizing out of our four-level house before moving to California, we planned for six weekends of "moving sales." To encourage new and repeat buyers, we created this info-sign with a box containing the latest listing of goods we brought out to sell. After our successful down-sizing, we finally reached the time to "sign off"!

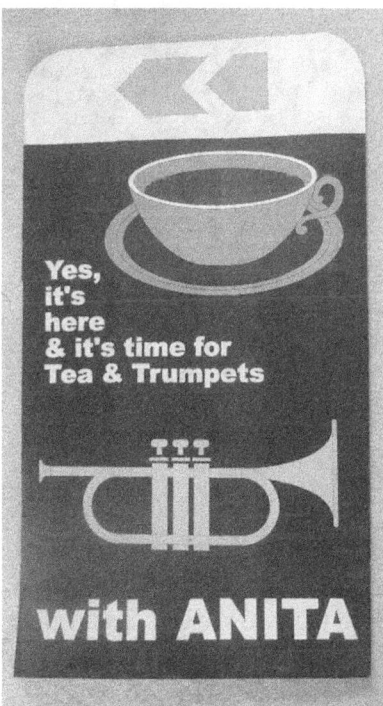

For **Anita**, too, the time had come to "sign off" from her work as a counselor at Lutheran Social Services in Tacoma.

Her colleagues at the office and other associates gathered for a special farewell for her at our church, Redeemer Lutheran in Fircrest.

While others organized the "goodbye" gathering, I prepared this "welcome" poster to greet folks coming to the event.

## Washington to California

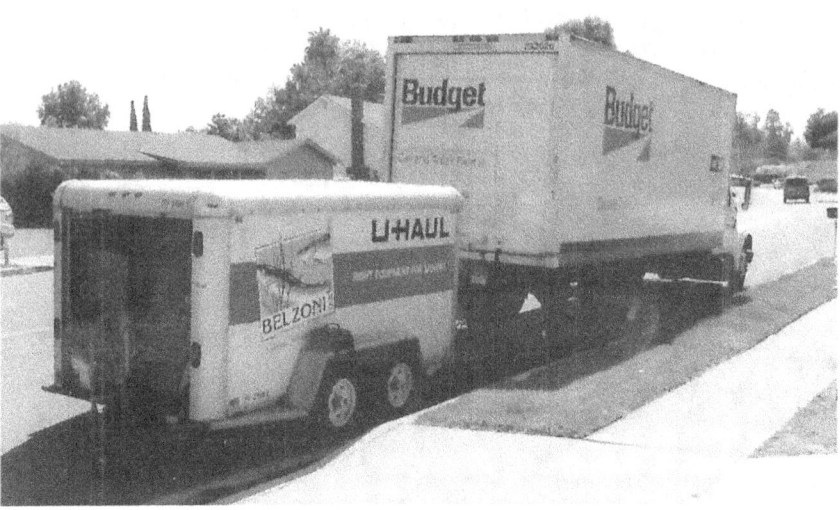

Despite our downsizing in Tacoma, we hauled a lot of stuff via our 1200-mile trek to Thousand Oaks. The contrast at right, between a contemporary light fixture in Thousand Oaks and a Tacoma decorative assemblage of wood, tells a story of change.

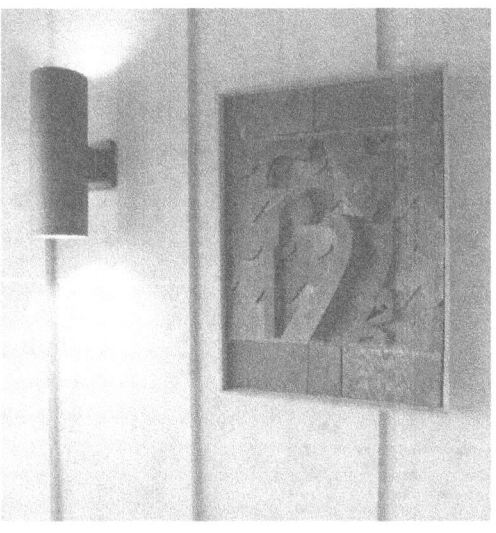

And the backdrop of **shingles** in this wood arrangement relates to my earliest apprenticeship…helping when we moved from one town to another…patching tires for our car and bikes…and **shingling** the roof and walls of our **Great Depression** house in Lynd, Minnesota.

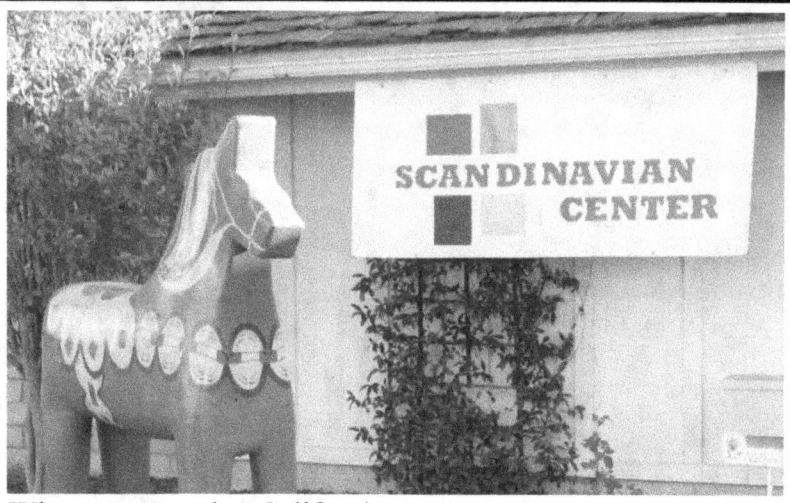

When we moved to California, we immediately connected with our Scandinavian links at California Lutheran University, where Anita and I now direct the Scandinavian Center. We "hitched up" the **Swedish Dala horse** (häst) shown here to invite "neigh-bors" to our meeting room, museum and library.

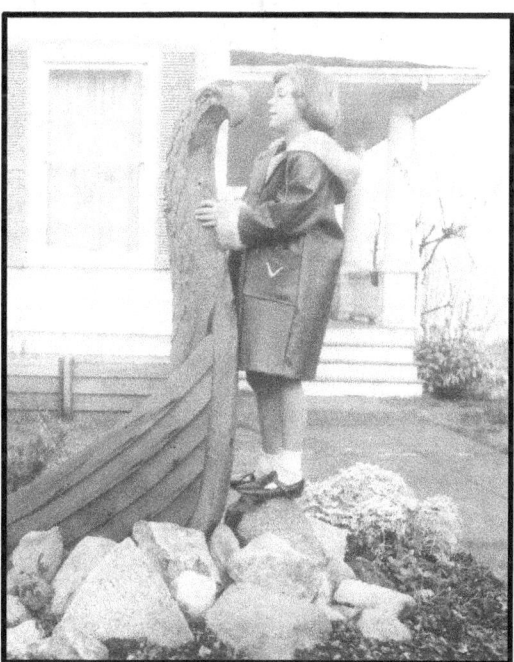

For part of our Nordic "greeting" to visitors at our new home in California, we salvaged our Viking ship "Sea Eagle" prow from Tacoma.

Earlier, our daughter Kristin consoled our Viking Sea Eagle, because obviously that ship had run aground on a rocky Puget Sound shore.

And we also posted this friendly Viking by the front door of the Scandinavian Center to imply "välkommen!"

So he "flew" again! I had recycled this sign from a discarded display formerly used by Scandinavian Airlines (SAS).

Eventually we used our Viking to advertise the **Scandinavian Festival,** one of the special events sponsored by our "parent organiztion":

# Scandinavian American Cultural and Historical Foundation, Inc. (SACHF).

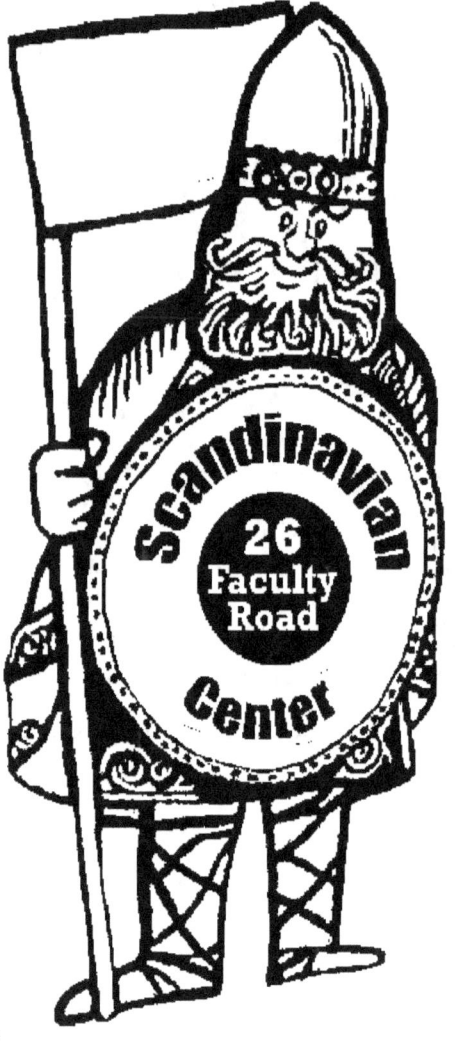

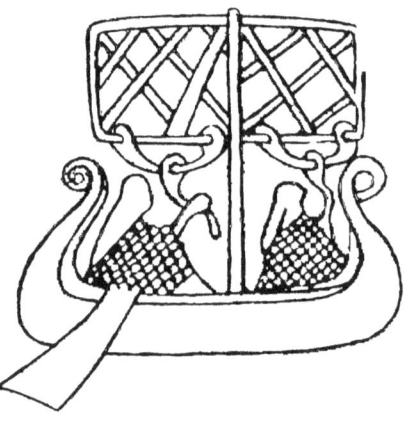

And we turned to the more-distant past to employ this Viking ship logo at left, drawn from Scandinavian antiquity.

My wife **Anita** initially served with me as a Director of the Scandinavian Center, but she also became President of the Scandinavian Cultural and Historical Foundation. Here she checks a "work in progress" of a model of a Norwegian stave church. Now, as

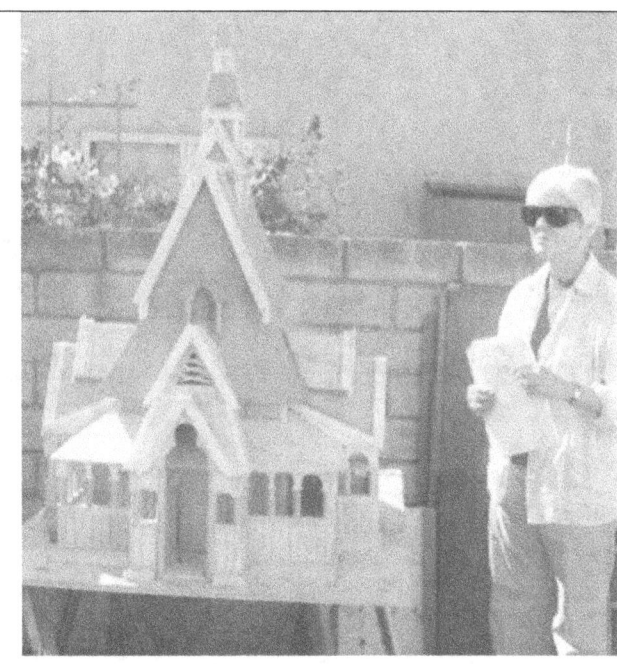

a finished display, it gets much attention from visitors.

As does the wooden goose hanging from the ceiling of the Scandinavian Center, with Nils Holgersson hanging on. That sign dominates the room with its 8' wingspan, and calls attenttion to the educational story here about Sweden, written by Selma Lagerlöf.

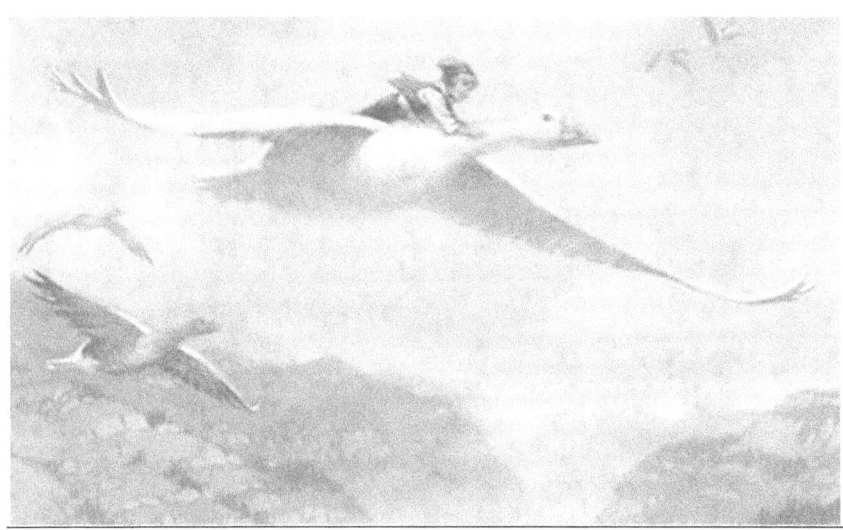

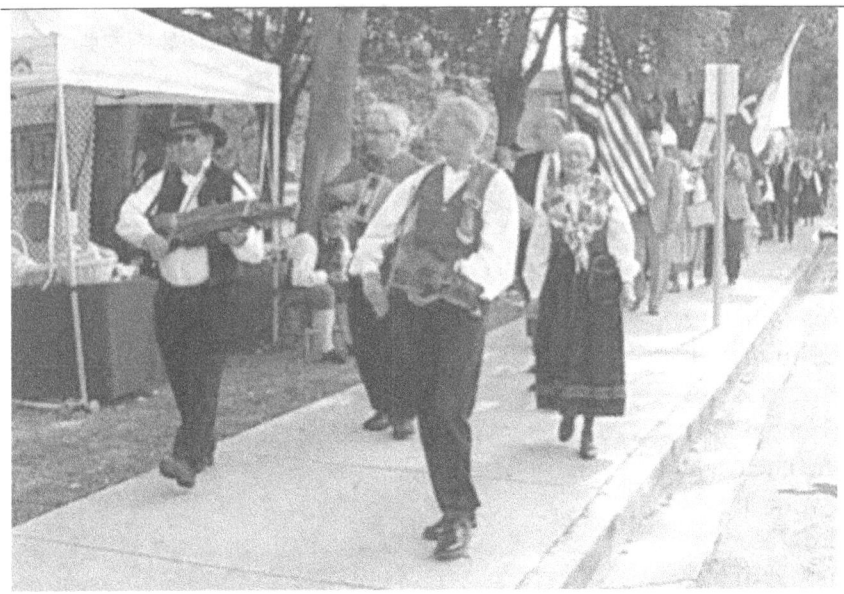

In her Norwegian costume, **Anita** (at right) marches in the parade to start the **Scandinavian Festival**, which attracts some 5,000 to Cal Lutheran as a major event of the Scandinavian American Cultural and Historical Foundation.

"If you can't fight City Hall"… take a display there, as Anita (below) did at the **Thousand Oaks Civic Center.**

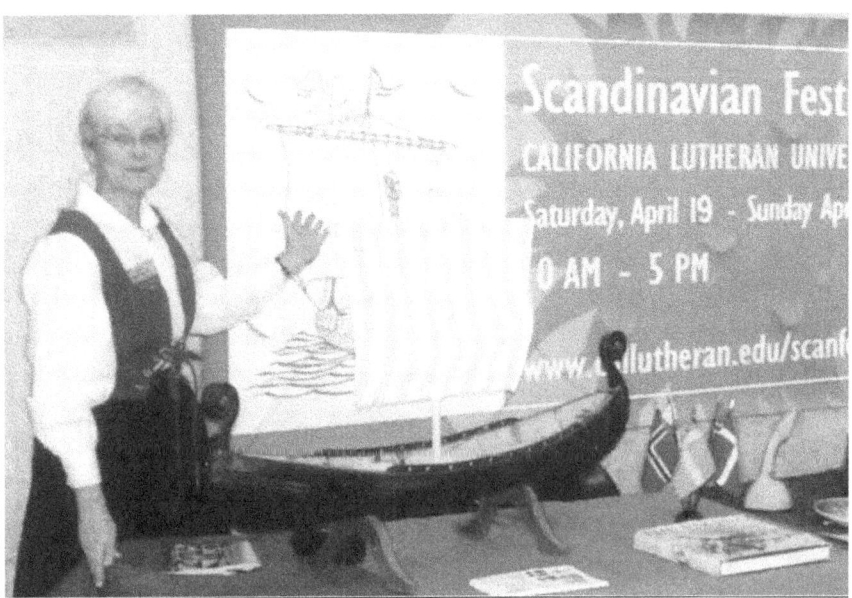

SACHF's **Nordic Spirit Symposium** explores academic topics annually in February. Meanwhile, the Scandinavian Center sponsors Scandinavian language classes, a book-discussion group, genealogy study and a gathering of lacemakers. The Center also houses a museum and an extensive library. And the Cal Lutheran Scandinavian Student Club and a class about Vikings meet there.

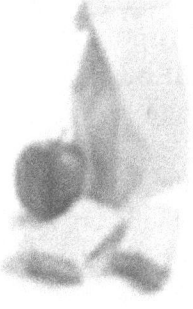 Meanwhile, the coffee (with snacks too) is always on for the FREE weekly **Brown-Bag Lunch** 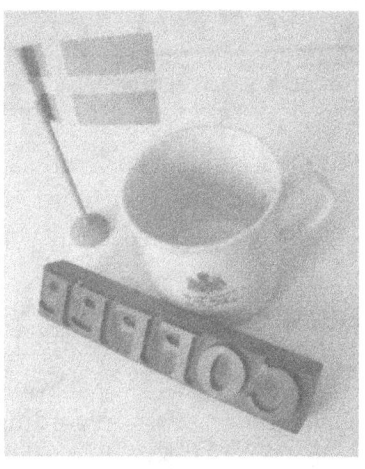 presentations, which are open to the public at the Center. The agenda includes a variety of Scandinavian-related topics and speakers.

For instance, the Brown-Bag Lunch photo below shows a **professor from UCLA** telling about the Swedish-American actor who portrayed Charlie Chan in the movies, and we learned about the professor's new book about the actor and the movie series.

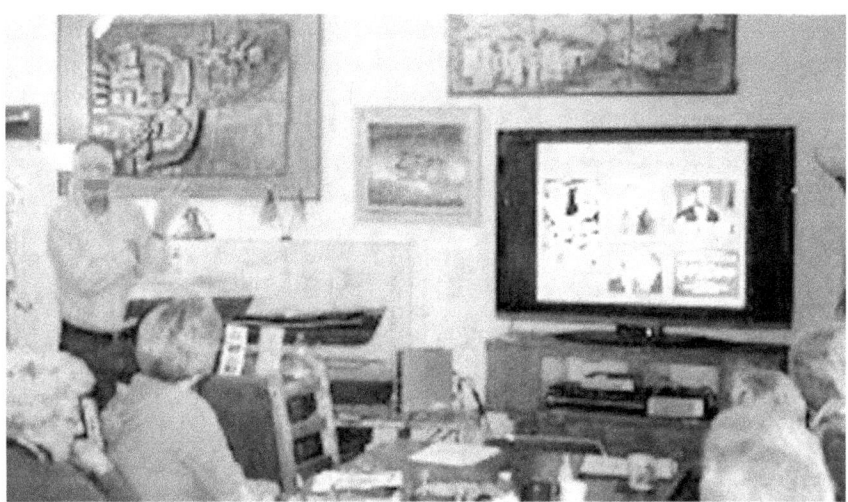

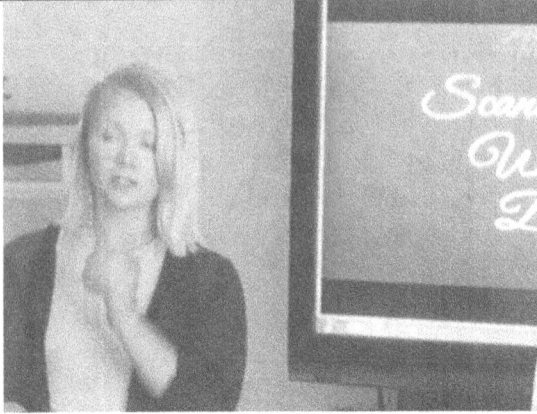

**California Lutheran University students** participate in several other ways as well, such as this student from a Norwegian organization speaking about her group during a Brown-Bag presentation.

Two other students as well as two from the Cal Lutheran faculty serve on the SACHF Board of Directors, and other members of the faculty and staff participate in various ways.

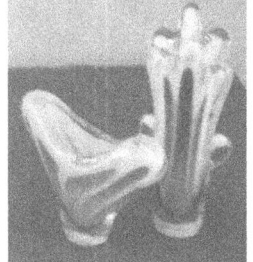

Many students assist with the Scandinavian Festival, while others take part as helpers in the Scandinavian Center library and by recording memberships and listing the donations of art (such as this Swedish glass), artifacts and books.

And our SACHF organization also supports the annual **Sankta Lucia** event (below), conducted by the student congregation in December in the chapel at California Lutheran University.

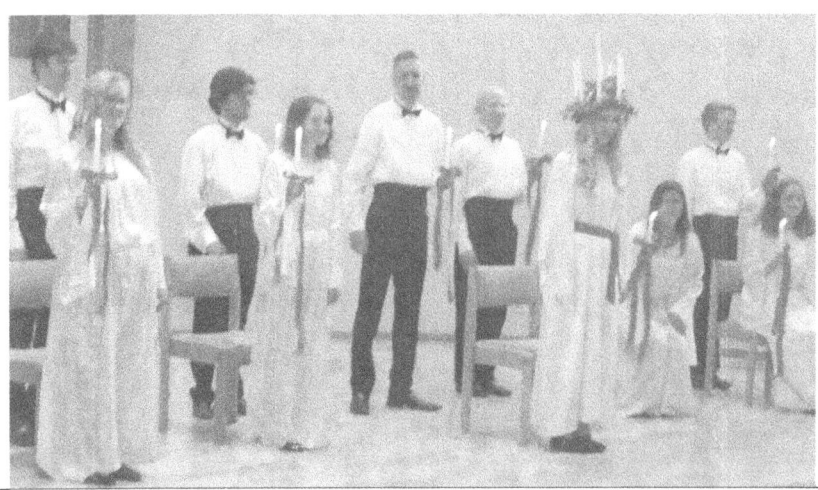

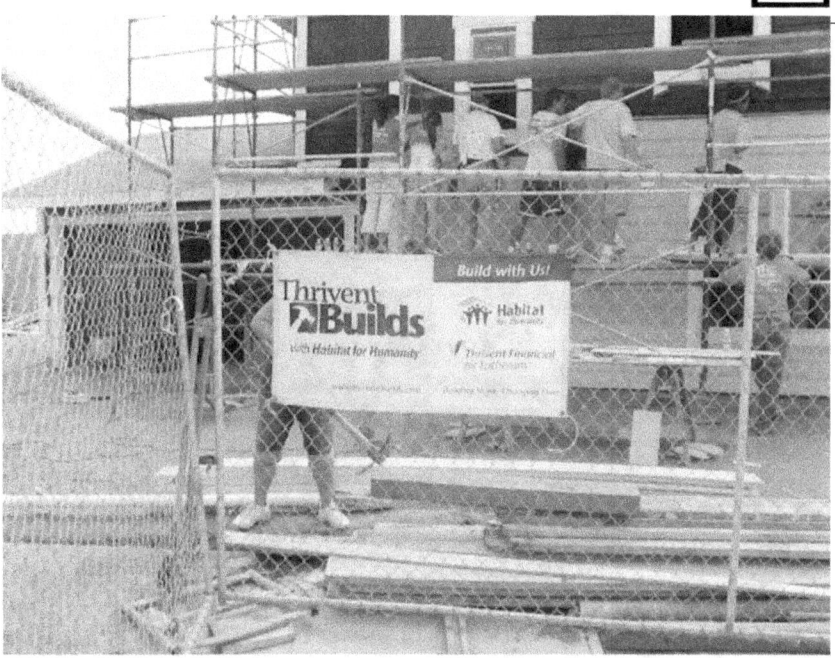

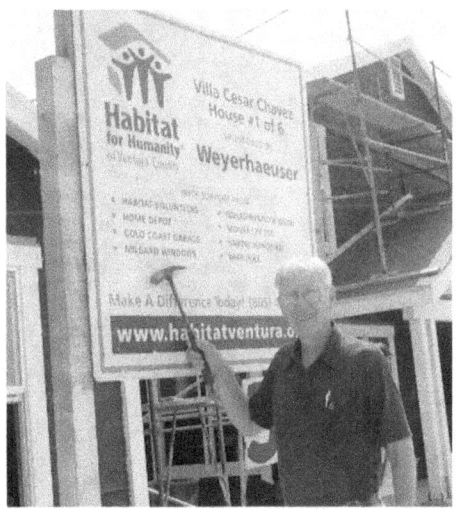

At a **Habitat** construction site (above) near Cal Lutheran, students and staff pitched in to help on a project supported by **Thrivent**, an investment program for Lutherans and other denominations.

As I photographed that project, I saw similar work next door—supported by **Weyerhaeuser** employees.

This **Habitat** involvement reminded me of our past in **Tacoma**, where our Thrivent branch sponsored Habitat construction and where a Weyerhaeuser executive led a multi-unit Habitat "build" of a cluster of new houses. That major endeavor and other "builds" also included participation of our congregation there as well as several more Lutheran and other churches.

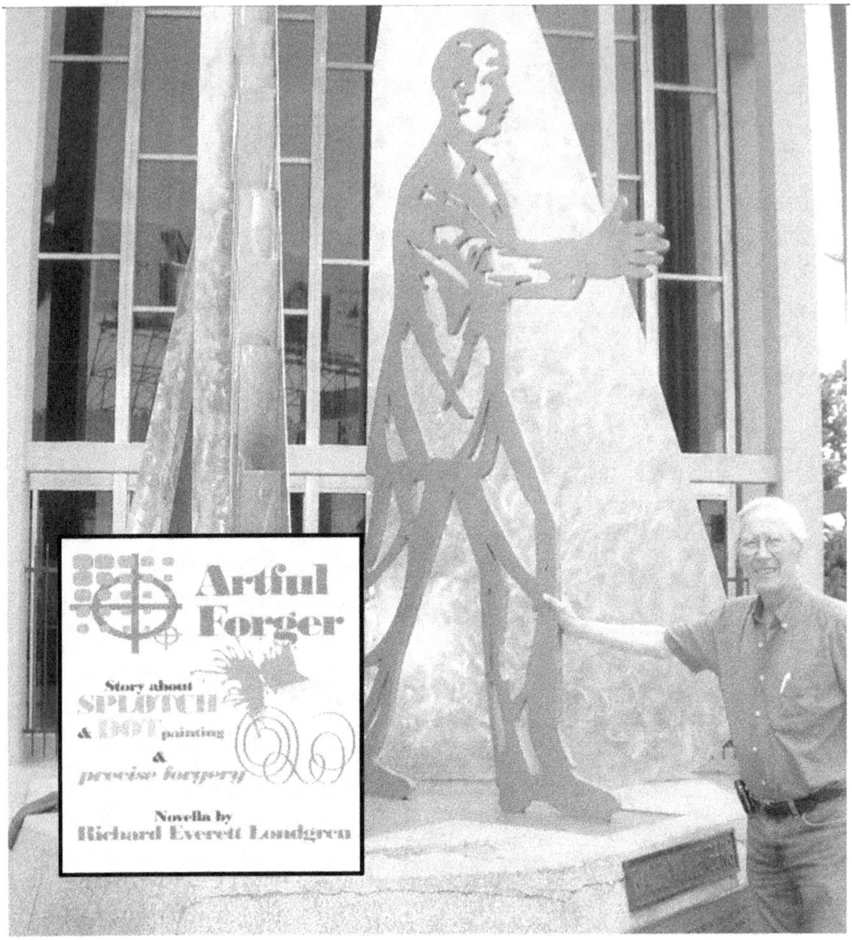

When we moved to California, we found plenty of architecture and art, including this distinctive "metal cutout" in Los Angeles that honors Sweden's **Raoul Wallenberg** for saving thousands of Jews from Nazi persecution during World War II. And the "Artful Forger" of my novel ▲ would get fictionally involved in that challenge by forging vital documents for those Jews.

Meanwhile, many museums have helped prepare us for our own museum leadership. Now in California, that learning continues. Here we can select from a variety of museums, of wide focus—art, cars, crafts, film, history and even printing. And we can drive just a few miles to visit the Reagan Library (museum). Plus going to many other local venues and events, including those on the campus of Cal Lutheran.

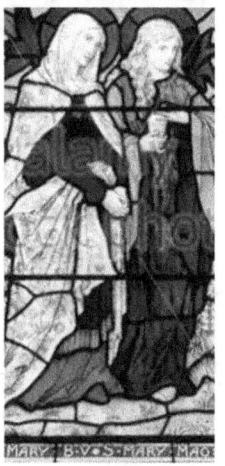

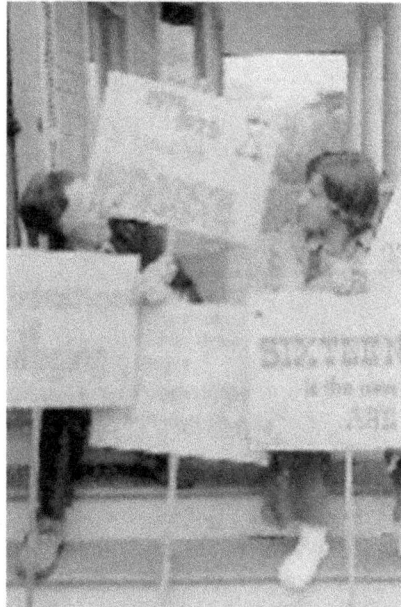

At Tacoma's First Lutheran, stained-glass windows like this decorated and helped teach, while later stained-glass was more symbolic. At another church in a different way of "teaching," our son Eric and I prepared a collection of signs to be shared as a friendly message in a "parade" during worship services.

## SignsZ of the changing TimeZ!

There I also taught a calligraphy class. For that, I produced the greeting here, employing a "dingbat" plus type to print a card to be used for a message lettered by members of our calligraphy class.

To promote that church's participation

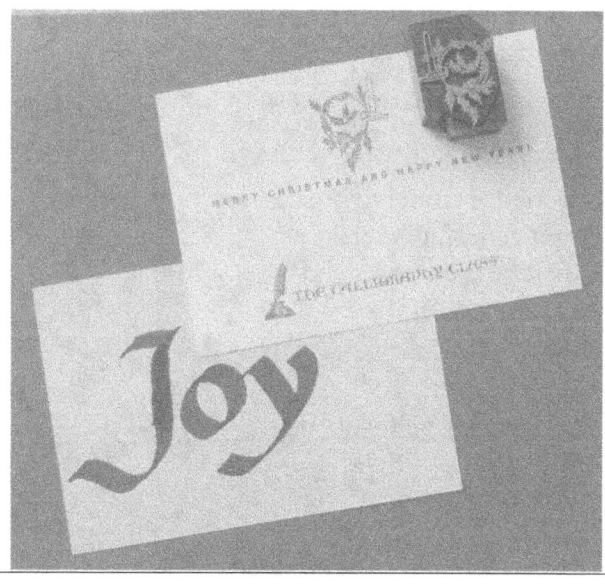

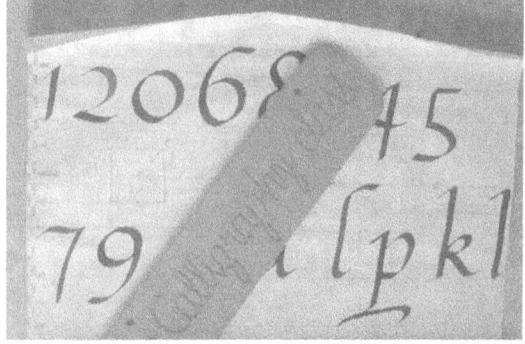

in new/old expression in a calligraphy class, I even created a bright-red sign with routed letters. I routed the script using the special tool (below) that I'd ordinarily use for carving printing blocks. The rolled-up chart is part of a series I prepared for teaching calligraphy, which I have usually supported with handouts (see page 43) giving the details of the letters, including the spacing and angles of the various letter forms.

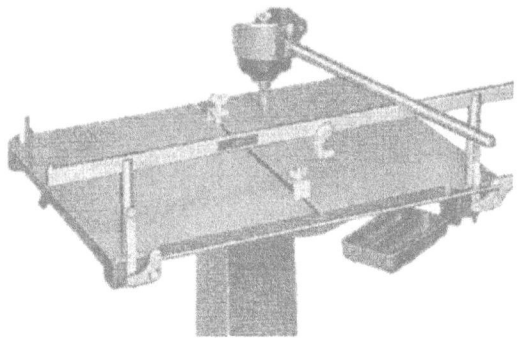

I prepared this circle and similar calligraphed forms for use in reports by our Lutheran congregation.

No, I didn't count on the level of skill and experience from anyone in our calligraphy class to handle the curves and various sizes of the letters.

Besides, this shape increased a calligraphy risk—misspelling.

*(What—no spell check?)*

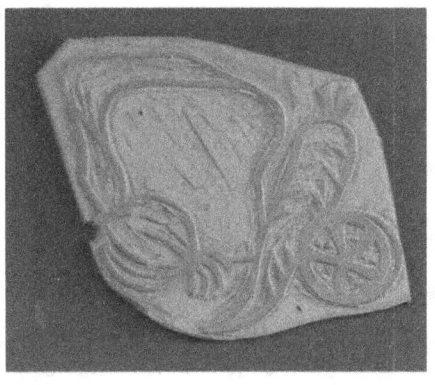 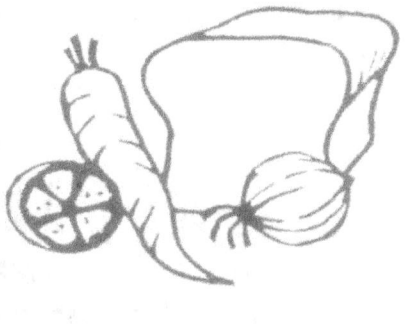

I printed this design on the cover of a cookbook that my wife Anita and others from First Lutheran Church published.

For the "printing plate" shown at left, I carved the design on a challenging block of hardboard, not the customary softer Linoleum block. At right: how our platen press printed it on the cover.

Their book called **POTLUCK** proved to be so popular, they ran out. And the recipes got possitive "feedback"!

Also in my "career of vounteerism," I for years served as a wide-ranging volunteer Lutheran communicator.

At one church as shown below, I counseled the leaders about their graphics. Because the church nestles in the business areas of the small city and in a location across from the local high school, I recommended a logo with a community setting—including an indication of a lighted football field.

My first camera, an Argus C3 I bought in Mankato, served me well initially while I wrote and edited regional Lutheran publications and contributed to our national Lutheran magazine as well.

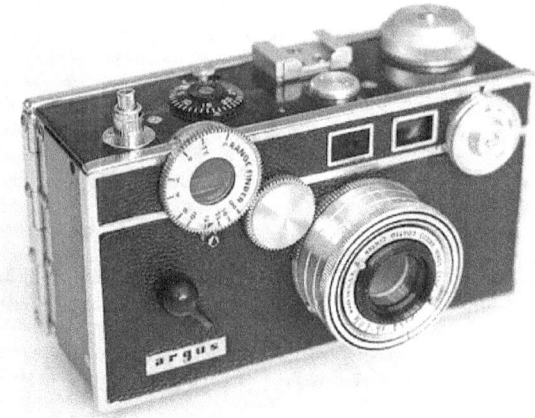

Eventually, I advanced to more sophisticated cameras, now with digital, of course. And a computer. I gained skill because I photographed for our company publications as well.

Later, I featured my Argus C3 as a primary "character" in a novel I wrote for Amazon.

The name of the novel, *Double Trouble,* relates to the double-exposure problem of the film not advancing automatically in this particular camera. Thus, a double-exposed film negative serves as a possible piece of evidence about a crime central to this story.

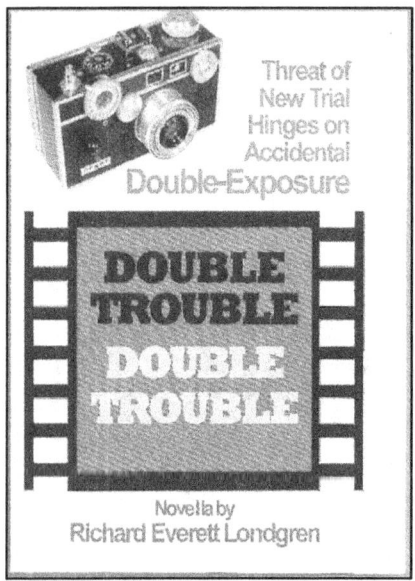

Threat of
New Trial
Hinges on
Accidental
Double-Exposure

DOUBLE
TROUBLE
DOUBLE
TROUBLE

Novella by
Richard Everett Londgren

The young woman in the novel, who serves as a school and community photographer, vaguely recalls in the story that the double-exposed negative—still hanging in her family's darkroom—might partially reveal significant details.

And that possibility forces a confession that's key to the conclusion.

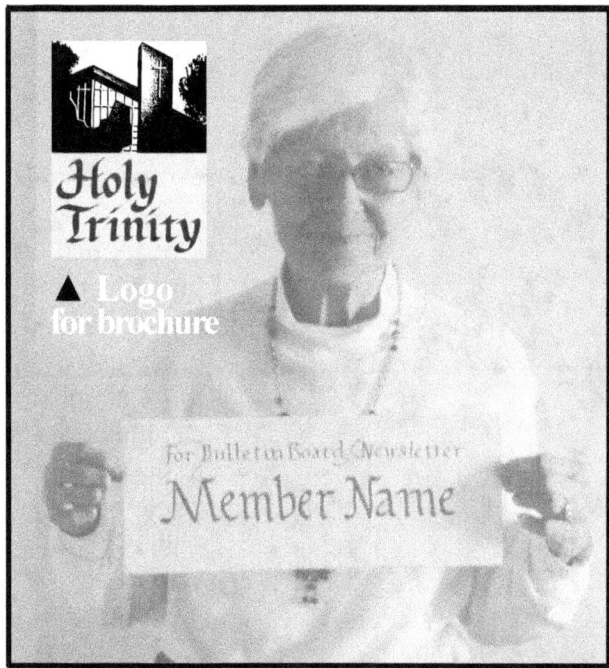

▲ Logo
for brochure

For Bulletin Board/Newsletter
Member Name

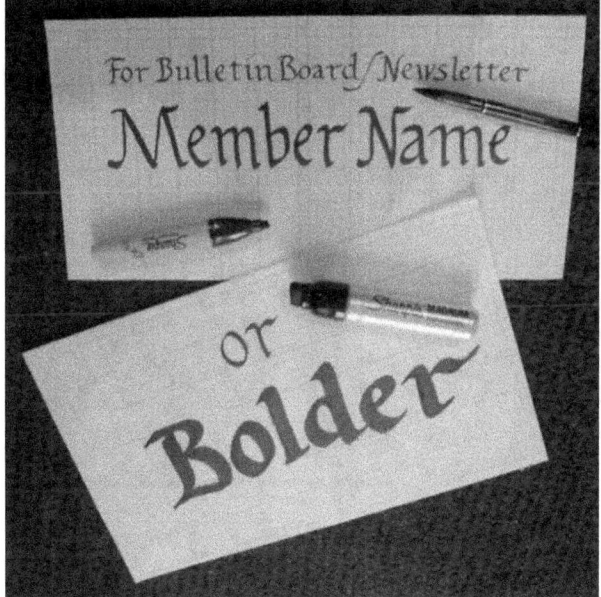

For Bulletin Board/Newsletter
Member Name

or
Bolder

I also employ photography to publicize new church members in our California congregation.

Simplifying the identification of the new members motivated me to letter the name of the person or family. Then, after I took the photo with the person's name included, I could provide it for the church bulletin board and newsletter.

During the photo "shoot," the subject or subjects and I would joke about registering them, like for a driver's license. Or?

I lettered the name/names on lined bookkeeping forms for easy sizing and alignment. Because I letter with an imprecise chisel-point Sharpie, I've developed a simple letter-form I call **Baltic Bold**.

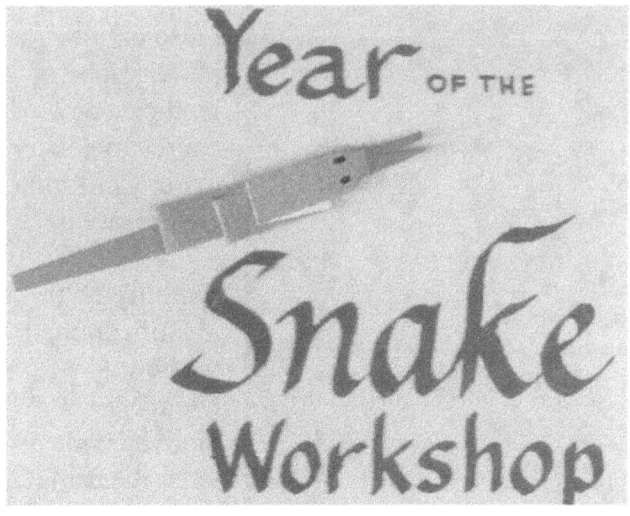

While producing a variety of church-related newsletters, I've applied my calligraphy for special uses, such as this example to call attention to the "Year of the Snake" (with its folded three-dimensional snake). And I've prepared "nameplates" for a variety of newsletters. Occasionally, I do add a bit of flourish to the usual plain letters.

*GME newsletter*

*NewsBites*

**Instead of hand-lettering, let the computer help with devices and type such as this to call attention to your special message.**

*Comic-strip dialogue can also work.*

In support of this "cottage industry" developed by women of Kenya, I prepared the "tall" logo showing giraffes, with the word "Kenya" added with my calligraphy.

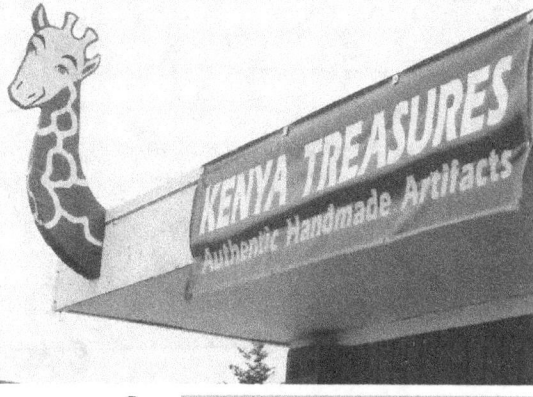

And here we go with another of my many "cutouts," as I created Ginny the Giraffe out of painted plywood.

By extending out from the sign on the front of the building, Ginny generates extra attention for the store.

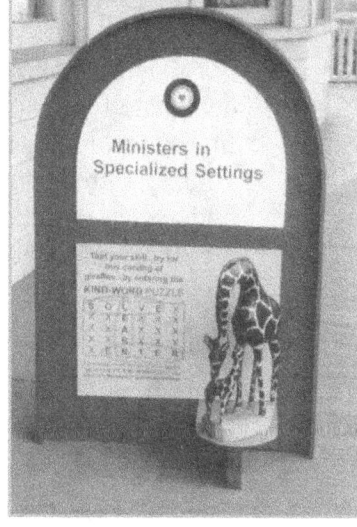

**A carved version of Ginny became an attention-getting prize in this Kind-Word puzzle I created for a Lutheran convention.**

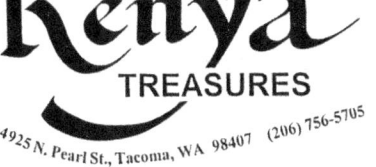

**TREASURES**

4925 N. Pearl St., Tacoma, WA 98407    (206) 756-5705

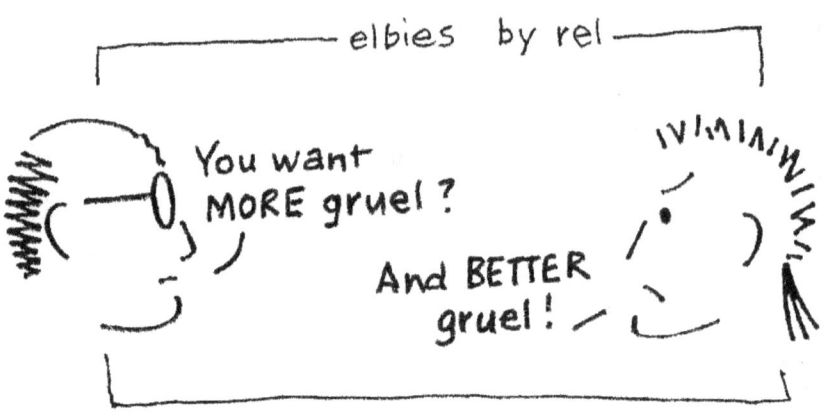

For meetings of a **Thrivent** committee established to designate funds for churches, schools and other not-for-profit organizations (such as **Habitat** noted before), I created a group of comic characters to underscore a pertinent message and to stimulate pleasant and meaningful discussion.

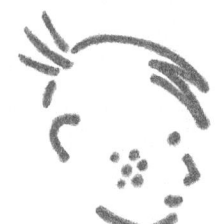

The "cast" of characters included male and female, young and older, and a mix of types.

**Kids too!**

**Now, all in favor of a bit of humor, say "aye!"**

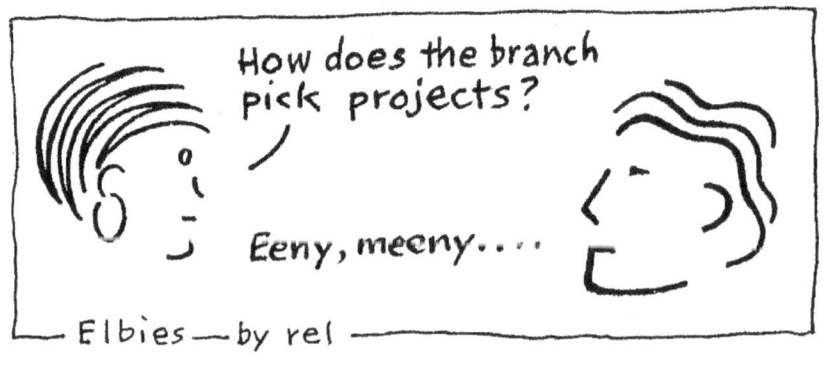

# Promotion SignZ

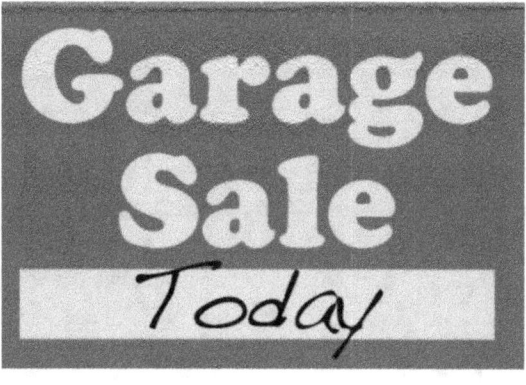

Stock "Garage Sale" signs can come from a variety of sources.

We made a set of five double-faced garage-sale signs, one for each corner of our block plus one at our house.

Reusable, and they were mounted on a wood stake, ready to be pounded into the ground (helped by my employing a long and pointed iron chisel to make a hole in the ground to avoid damaging the top of the stake by excessive hammering).

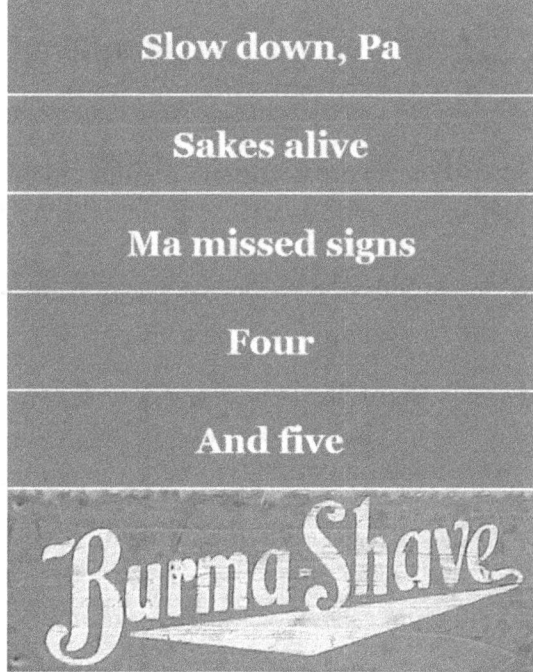

Slow down, Pa

Sakes alive

Ma missed signs

Four

And five

Our calligraphed bold signs got much positive attention—and business too.

But not quite like the impact of the old **Burma-Shave** series of signs (as shown at left) I saw when I was a kid. Now their appeal might be considered a driver distraction… and banned from the roadside.

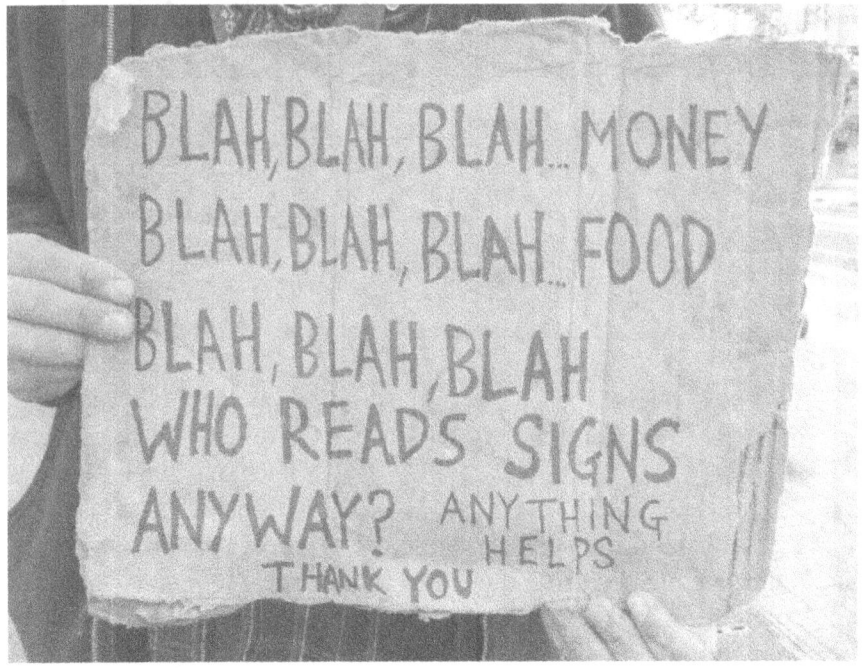

Now when we see the crude cardboard hand-lettered signs at exits out of shopping areas, we notice how similar they all seem.

Makes us wonder whether some support-agency produces them in volume to share for street-corner appeals.

Possibly a silk-screener has produced sets of the signs and made them available.

Our answer to such an appeal would be to advise the person in need to take advantage of the meals and housing provided by organizations of churches, including ours.

In answer to requests for gas money, some church organizations have even arranged for a one-time "credit card" to be given with value usable for a certain amount of gas at a nearby station.

# Alphabet OptionZ

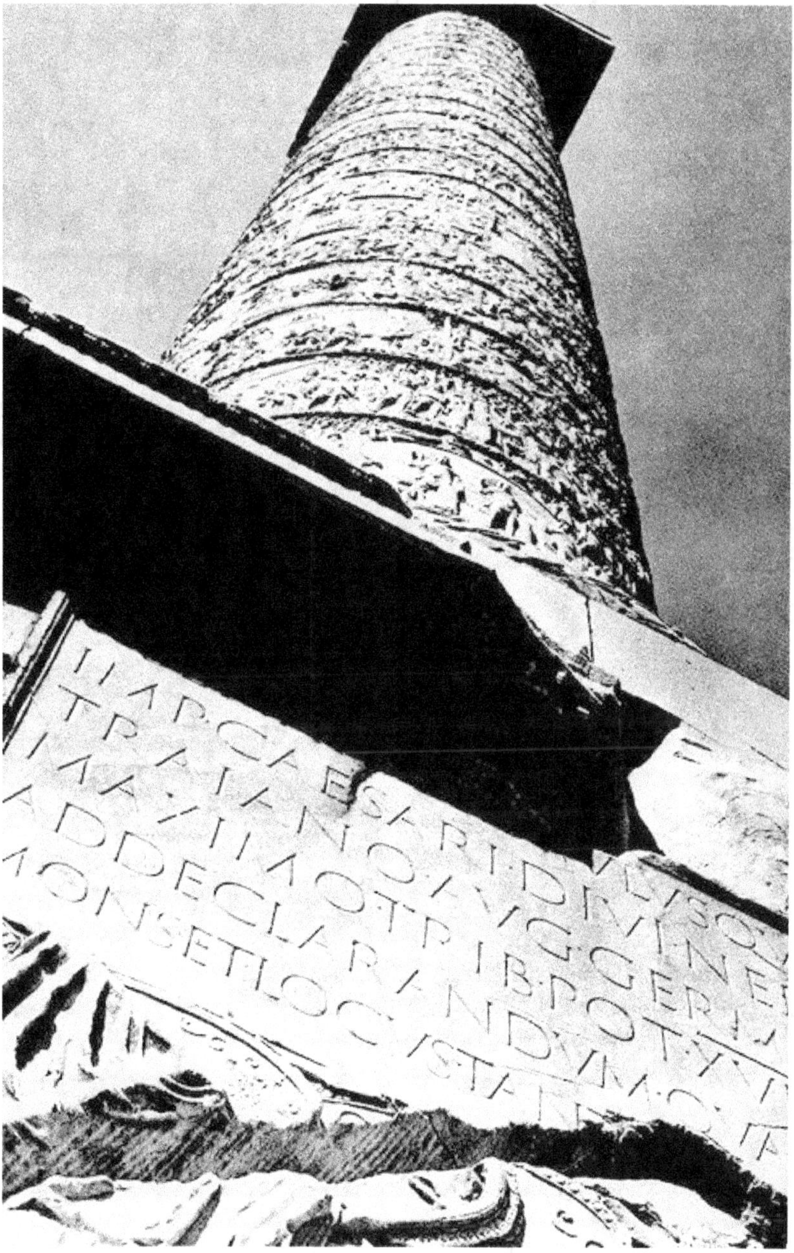

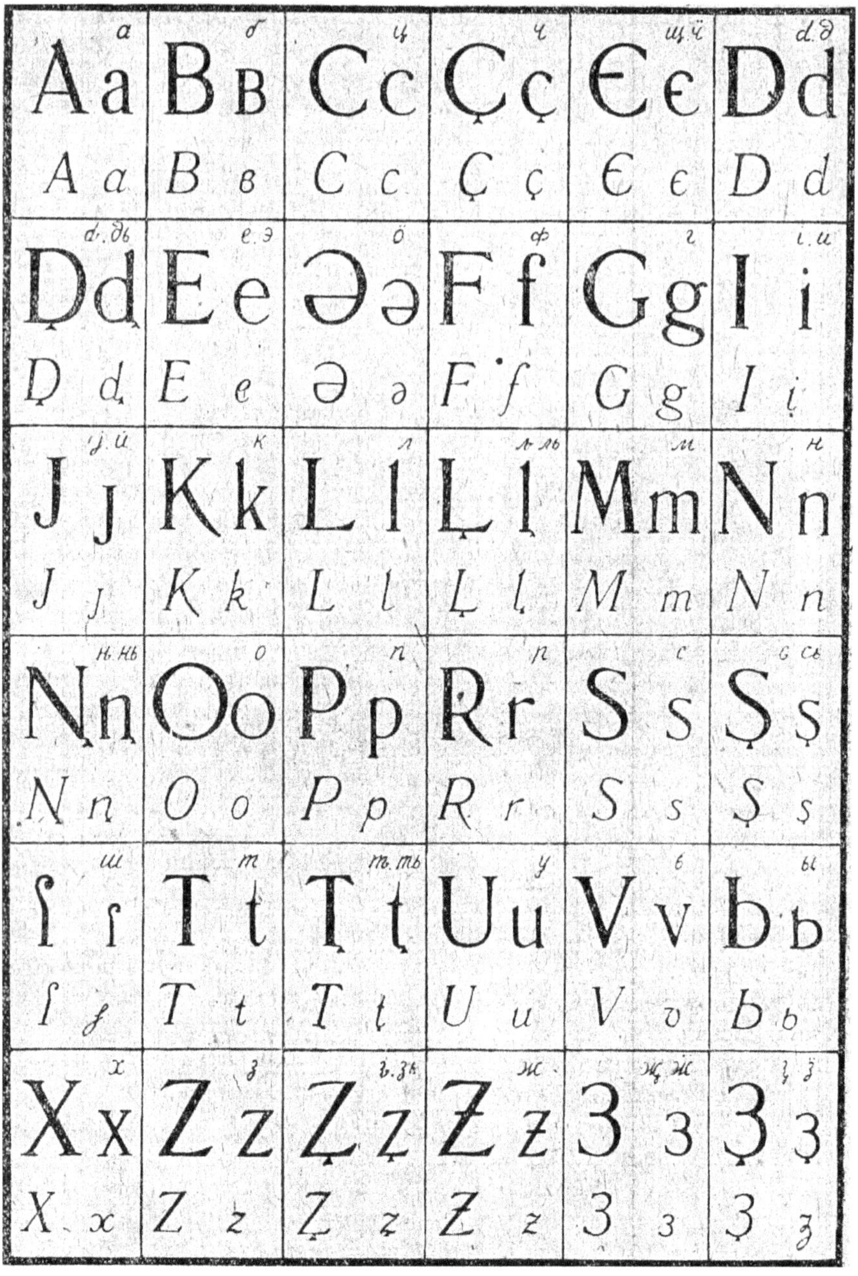

| a | б | ч | ч | щ,ч | d.ә |
|---|---|---|---|---|---|
| Aa | Bв | Cc | Çç | Єє | Dd |
| A a | B в | C c | Ç ç | Є є | D d |

| d.дб | е.э | о | ф | г | і.и |
|---|---|---|---|---|---|
| Dd | Ee | Әә | Ff | Gg | Ii |
| D d | E e | Ә ә | F f | G g | I i |

| j.й | к | л | л.ль | м | н |
|---|---|---|---|---|---|
| Jj | Kk | Ll | Ļl | Mm | Nn |
| J j | K k | L l | Ļ l | M m | N n |

| н.нь | о | n | n | с | ѕ.сь |
|---|---|---|---|---|---|
| Ņn | Oo | Pp | Rr | Ss | Şş |
| Ņ n | O o | P p | R r | S s | Ş ş |

| ш | т | т.ть | у | в | ы |
|---|---|---|---|---|---|
| ſſ | Tt | Țț | Uu | Vv | bb |
| ſ ſ | T t | Ț ț | U u | V v | b b |

| х | з | з.зь | ж | ж.жь | ҙ.з |
|---|---|---|---|---|---|
| Xx | Zz | Ƶƶ | Żż | Зз | Ҙҙ |
| X x | Z z | Ƶ ƶ | Ż ż | З з | Ҙ ҙ |

This Roman alphabet relates to the letters on the Trajan Column, though these demonstrate the thick-and-thin shape plus serifs.

## Roman Numeral Table

| | | | | | | | |
|---|---|---|---|---|---|---|---|
| 1 | I | 14 | XIV | 27 | XXVII | 150 | CL |
| 2 | II | 15 | XV | 28 | XXVIII | 200 | CC |
| 3 | III | 16 | XVI | 29 | XXIX | 300 | CCC |
| 4 | IV | 17 | XVII | 30 | XXX | 400 | CD |
| 5 | V | 18 | XVIII | 31 | XXXI | 500 | D |
| 6 | VI | 19 | XIX | 40 | XL | 600 | DC |
| 7 | VII | 20 | XX | 50 | L | 700 | DCC |
| 8 | VIII | 21 | XXI | 60 | LX | 800 | DCCC |
| 9 | IX | 22 | XXII | 70 | LXX | 900 | CM |
| 10 | X | 23 | XXIII | 80 | LXXX | 1000 | M |
| 11 | XI | 24 | XXIV | 90 | XC | 1600 | MDC |
| 12 | XII | 25 | XXV | 100 | C | 1700 | MDCC |
| 13 | XIII | 26 | XXVI | 101 | CI | 1900 | MCM |

This arrangement of Arabic numbers relating to corresponding Roman numerals brings out an interesting contrast, because Americans, for example, have not found Roman numerals to "roll off the tongue" (so to speak) easily, so the Arabic numbers seem to serve us better.

On the other hand (or foot), the English system of measurement prevails here, though the metric system makes more sense.

And in language, we revolted against much British spelling of basic words.

Just no accounting for taste!

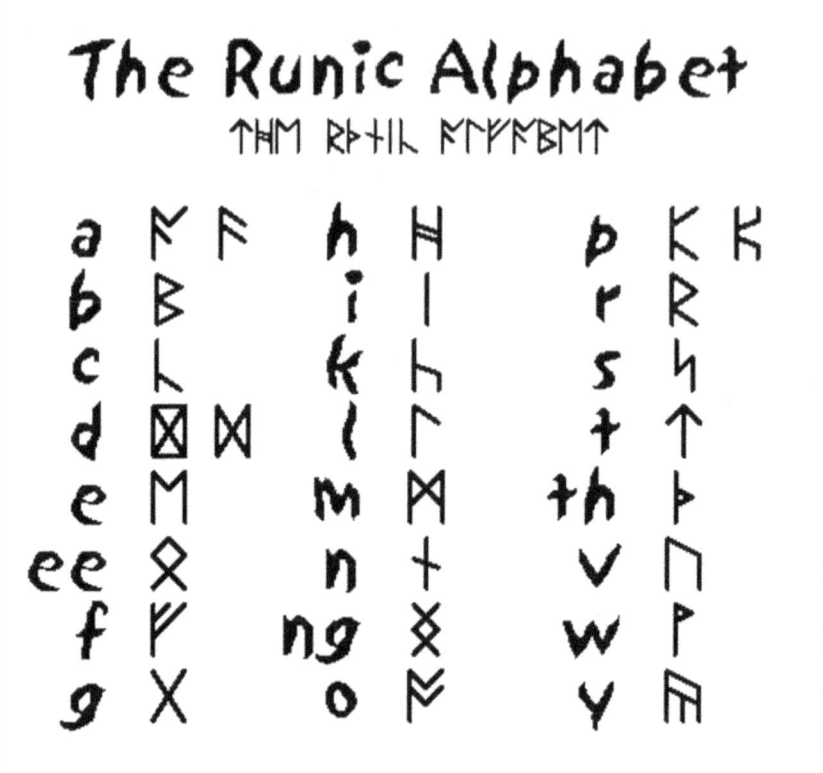

# The Runic Alphabet

| | | | | | | | | |
|---|---|---|---|---|---|---|---|---|
| a | ᛘ ᚠ | | h | ᚻ | | þ | ᚲ ᚴ |
| b | ᛒ | | i | ᛁ | | r | ᚱ |
| c | ᚴ | | k | ᚴ | | s | ᛋ |
| d | ⊠ ᛗ | | l | ᚱ | | t | ↑ |
| e | ᛗ | | m | ᛘ | | th | ᚦ |
| ee | ◇ | | n | ᛏ | | v | ᚢ |
| f | ᚡ | | ng | ⊗ | | w | ᚹ |
| g | ᚷ | | o | ᛟ | | y | ᛮ |

Above, the Scandinavian and other Germanic-related language at one time featured these primitive **runic** letter forms.

Runes seem to vary considerably, matched to certain sections of the area.

Runic carvings on stones and huge boulders show up as markers of people and accomplishments, especially in Sweden.

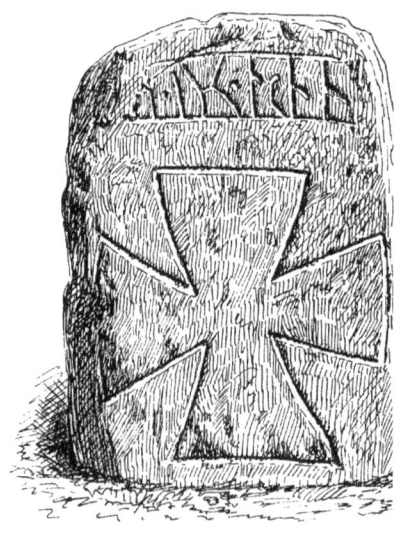

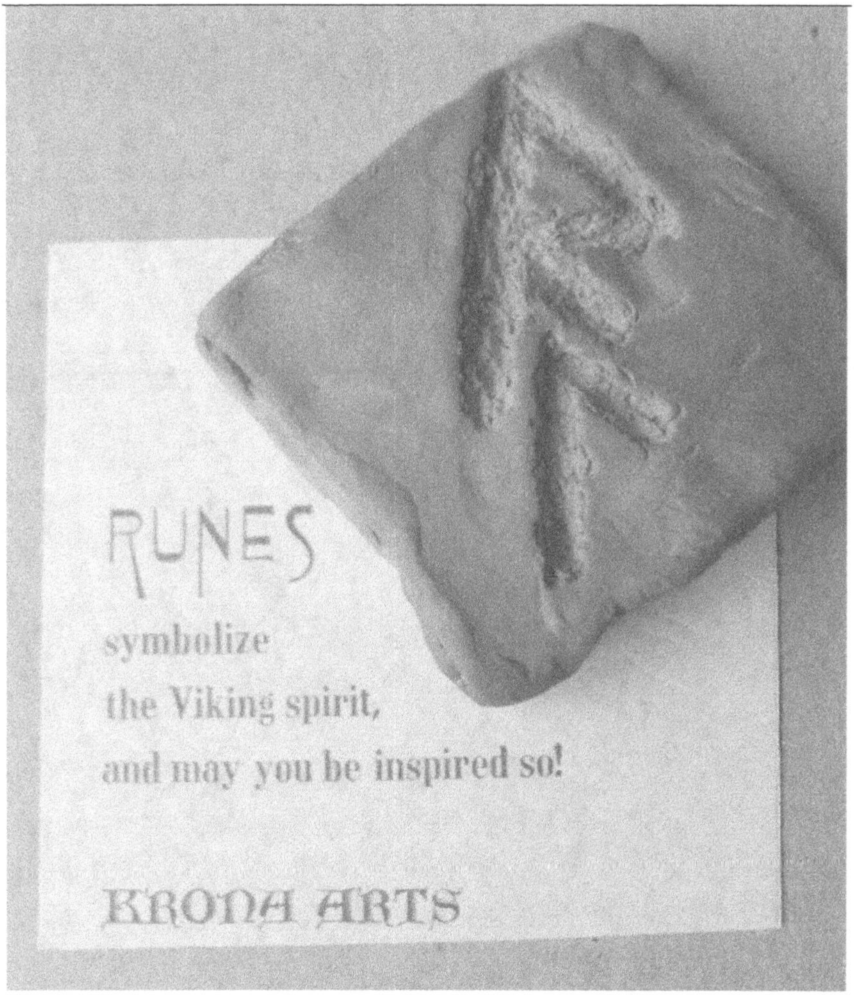

RUNES

symbolize
the Viking spirit,
and may you be inspired so!

KRONA ARTS

I created my personal **rune** with my RL initials set in clay, resting on a form I printed on our Krona Press. The next page shows a print titled "**Danegeld**" that relates to gold paid to keep the Vikings out of Paris. The French had paid the "gold" in the form of turning over Normandy to the threatening invaders. Later, **Winston Churchill** declared to the Nazis that England did not intend to pay Danegeld in protection money.

For the runic title of the Danegeld print, I carved the runes out of a Linoleum block. For the Viking-ships printing blocks, I sawed hardboard shapes (however, the shapes were not used in that "decorative" arrangement for the printing of the poster).

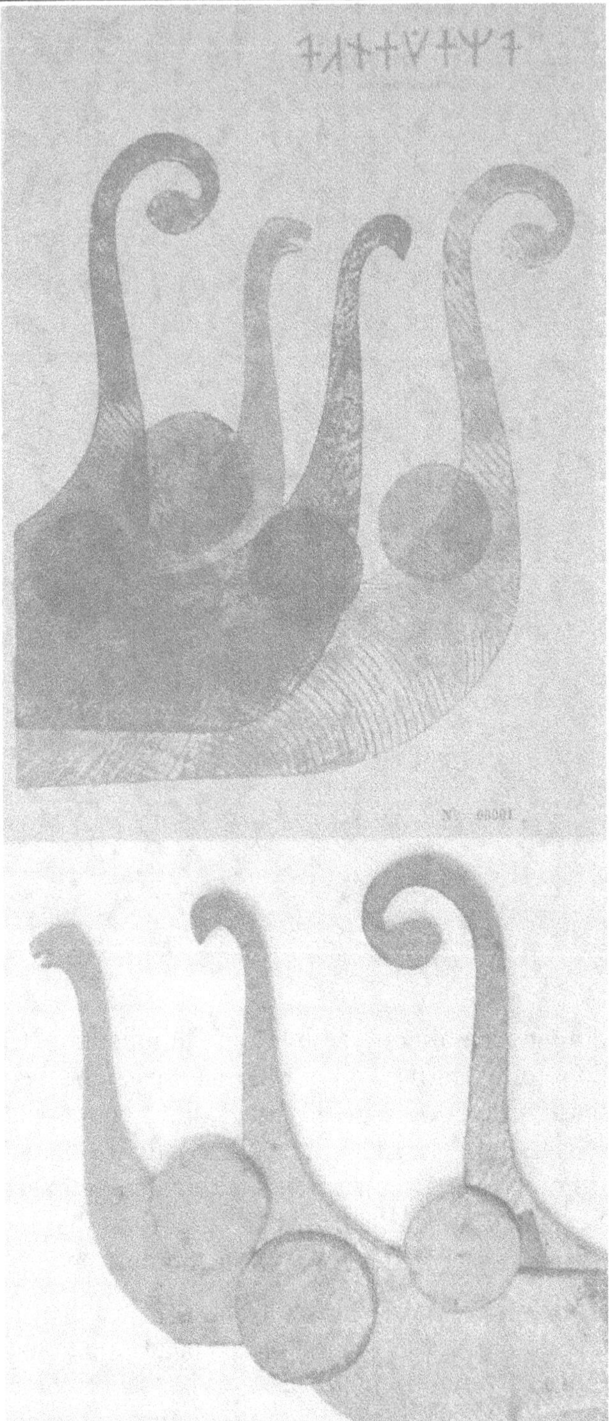

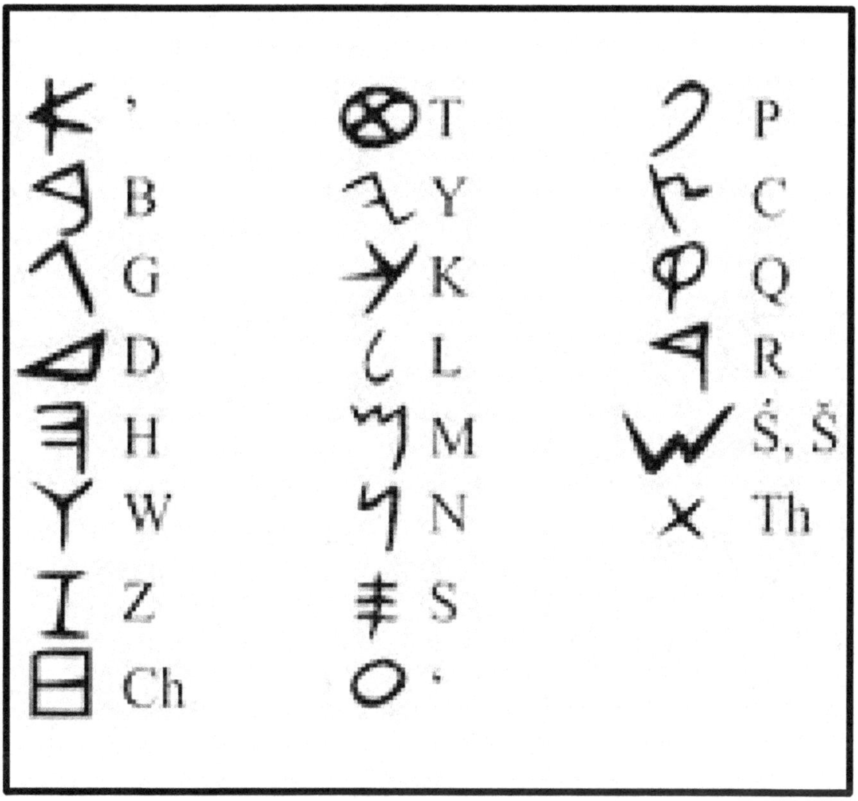

| | | | | | |
|---|---|---|---|---|---|
| 𐤀 | ' | 𐤈 | T | 𐤐 | P |
| 𐤁 | B | 𐤉 | Y | 𐤑 | C |
| 𐤂 | G | 𐤊 | K | 𐤒 | Q |
| 𐤃 | D | 𐤋 | L | 𐤓 | R |
| 𐤄 | H | 𐤌 | M | 𐤔 | Ś, Š |
| 𐤅 | W | 𐤍 | N | 𐤕 | Th |
| 𐤆 | Z | 𐤎 | S | | |
| 𐤇 | Ch | 𐤏 | · | | |

Even though the **Phoenician ships**
(as explained on the next page) sailed long before the **Viking
ships**, the resemblance between the designs seems like an
amazing coincidence. Or maybe some of the Phoenician designs,
including their **alphabet and letter-forms**, migrated north as the
Phoenicians reputedly journeyed that way to acquire the amber
available in the Baltic Sea area.

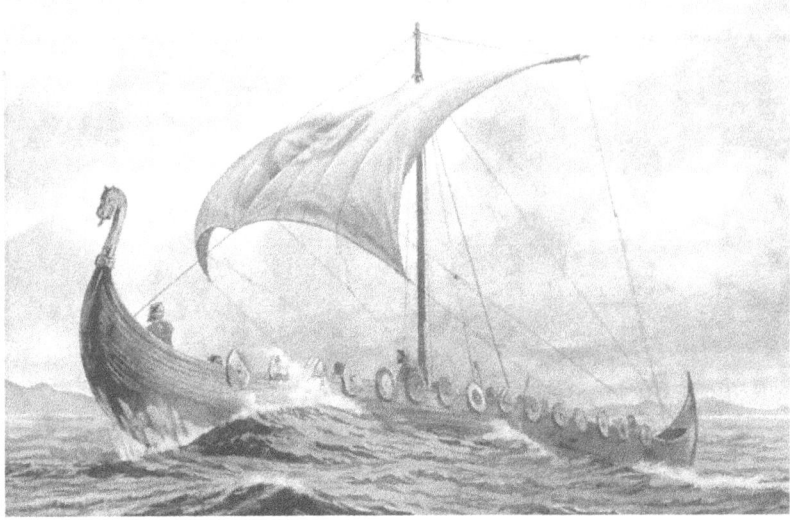

With surprisingly similar ships as noted, the **Viking**s (above) and the **Phoenicians** (below) sailed far from home base: the Vikings reached the Mediterranean, while the Phoenicians may have gone north to the Baltic. Both groups became outstanding traders, though the Phoenicians plied the seas a thousand years earlier.

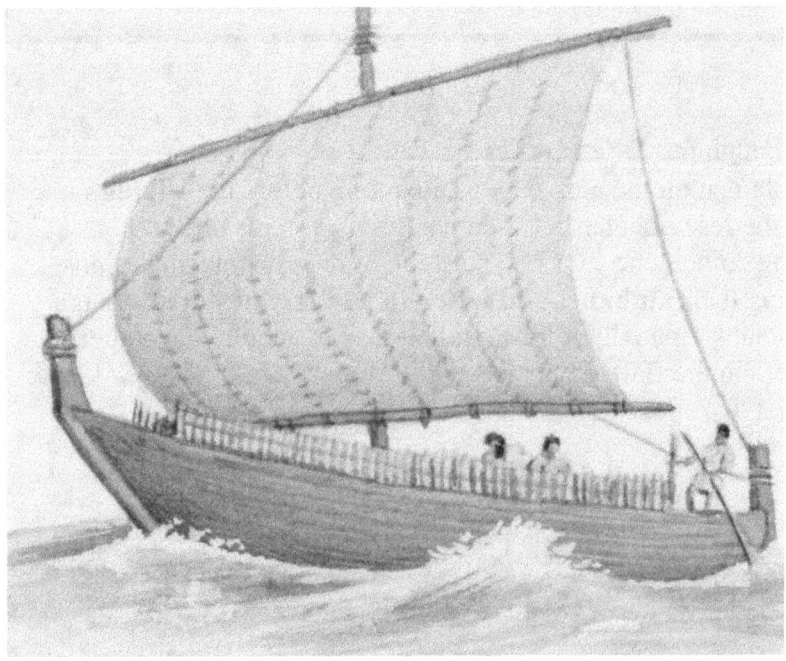

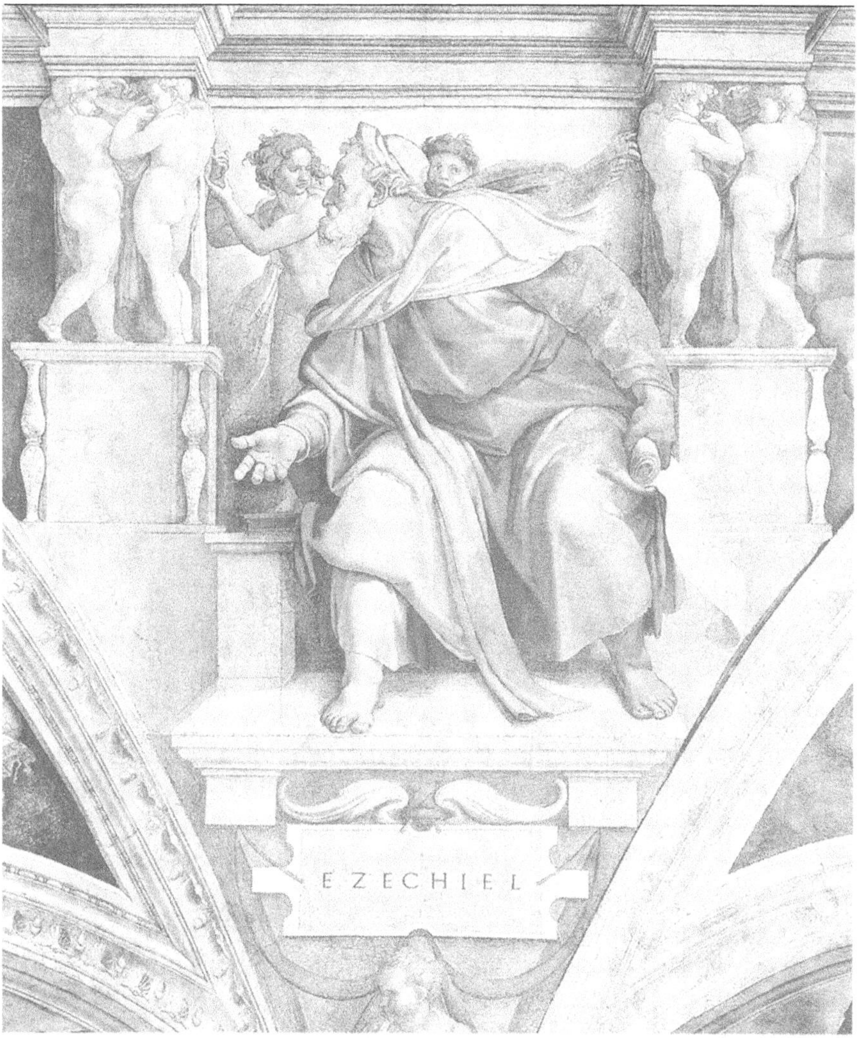

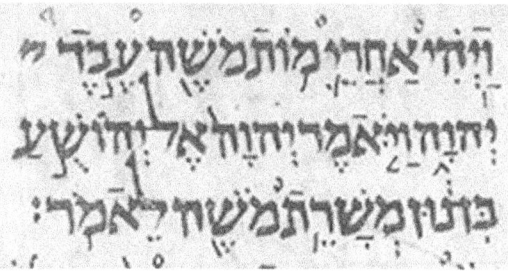

As indicated here in the painting in the Sistine Chapel by **Michelangelo** of **Ezechiel,** who was among others in the Old Testament who wrote about the seafaring Phoenicians and their impact in spreading God's story across the Mediterranean Sea and possibly beyond that reach as well.

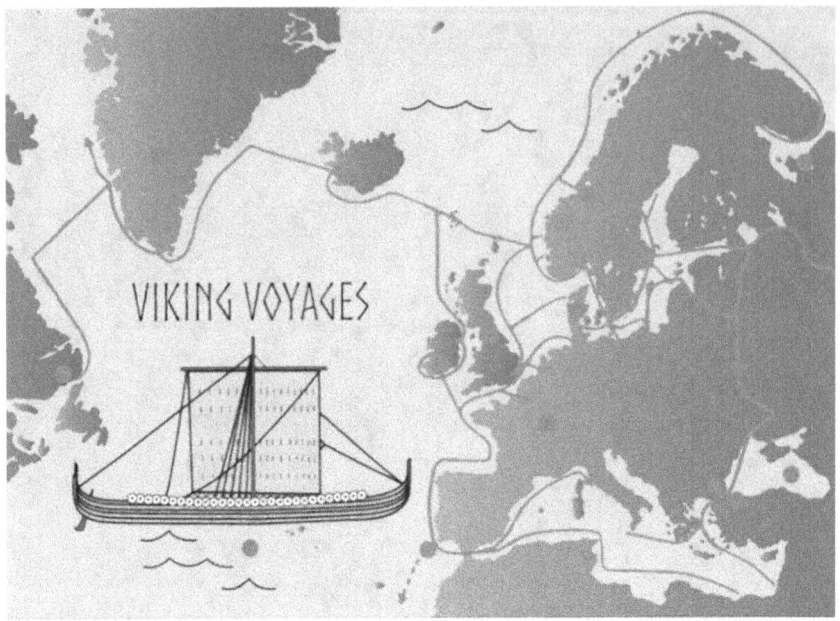

Writings such as the Viking **Sagas** and *Anglo-Saxon Chronicle* plus crude maps earlier than this version help tell the story of the ventures and settlements of the Scandinavians in their extended outreach in their world circa 1000.

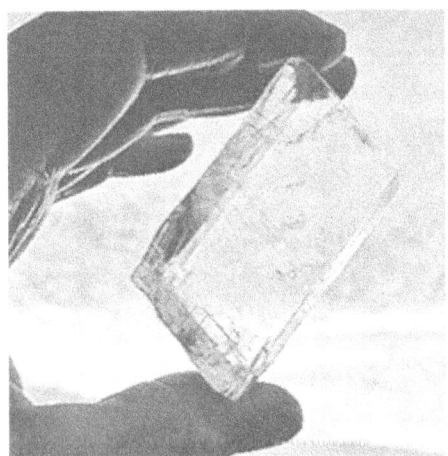

In navigating their world, the Vikings got help from a primitive polarizing device, a simple magnetic compass and a special sun-tracking tool.

But how about the globe hanging in our Country School? And the "pull-down" maps like window shades? And the reshaping of the world in the "orange-peel" map?

## SignZ of changing ToolZ!

# Readable Writing

**Michelangelo** would have understood the importance of creating letters big enough on the ceiling of the Sistine Chapel to be literally readable, but I don't know if he had a gauge like the letter-sizing chart below. Equally important is the reminder to make your message figuratively readable and understandable, as I've urged over and over in my book *Communication by Objectives.*

| LETTER HEIGHT | READABLE DISTANCE FOR MAXIMUM IMPACT | MAXIMUM READABLE DISTANCE |
|---|---|---|
| 1" | 10' | 30' |
| 2" | 20' | 60' |
| 3" | 30' | 90' |
| 5" | 50' | 150' |
| 7" | 70' | 210' |
| 10" | 100' | 300' |
| 12" | 120' | 360' |
| 15" | 150' | 450' |
| 18" | 180' | 540' |
| 24" | 240' | 720' |
| 30" | 300' | 900' |

As noted before, the serifs and the thick-and-thin letters do help the eye in reading. The same might be said about the value of capital letters used in combination with the lower-case letters.

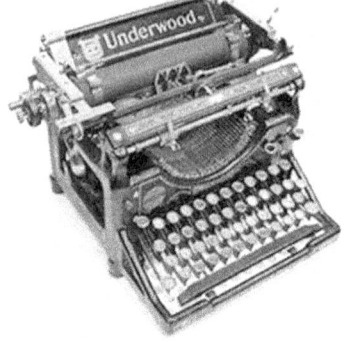

I learned to type on an old manual typewriter, like this. In the traditional "qwerty" arrangement of the keys. Of course, I did have to shift the type for capital letters.

**DING!** Time to advance the paper—manually.

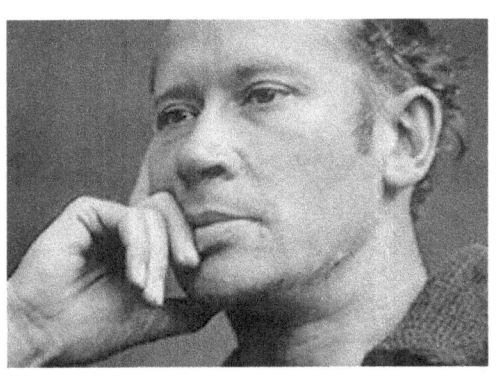

The poet **e e cummings**, for instance, disdained capital letters in an approach that might add distinction among the literati but cause distraction for most readers—such as we who need all the reading help we can get.

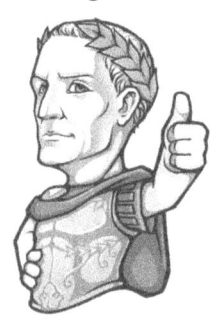

Of course, in our age of the Internet, capital letters do complicate typing (keyboarding) in many contemporary applications.

But the Romans since the times of Trajan signaled messages the way demonstrated at left, leading to symbols that now help speed up and enhance our current communication.

So, through "thick and thin," we should be able to carry on!

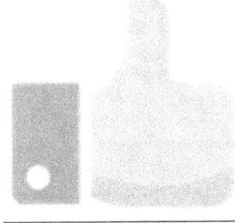

Certainly **signZ of the timeZ!**

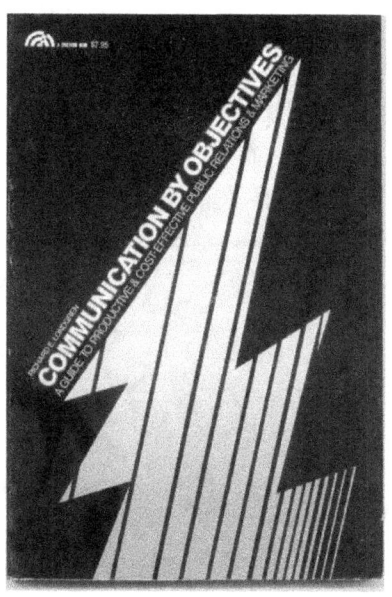

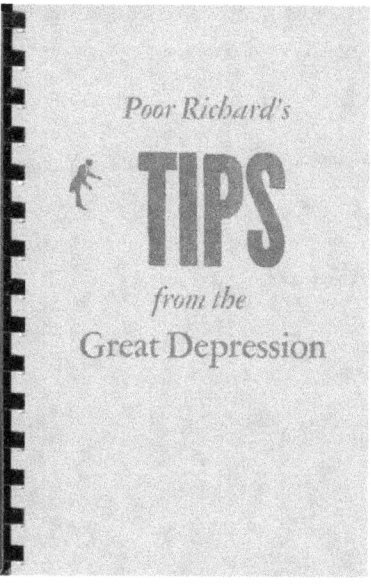

Poor Richard's

**TIPS**

*from the*

Great Depression

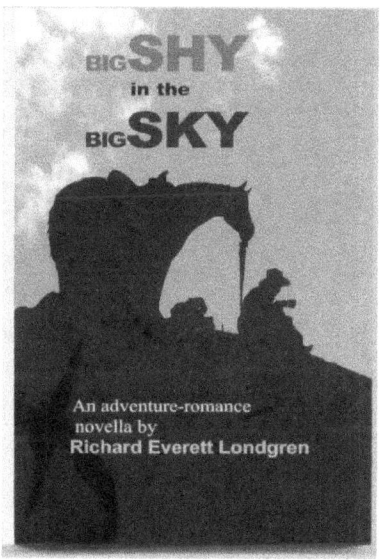

BIG**SHY**
in the
BIG**SKY**

An adventure-romance
novella by
Richard Everett Londgren

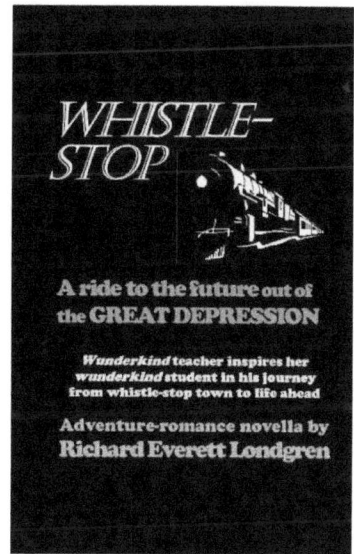

*WHISTLE-STOP*

A ride to the future out of
the GREAT DEPRESSION

*Wunderkind* teacher inspires her
*wunderkind* student in his journey
from whistle-stop town to life ahead

Adventure-romance novella by
**Richard Everett Londgren**

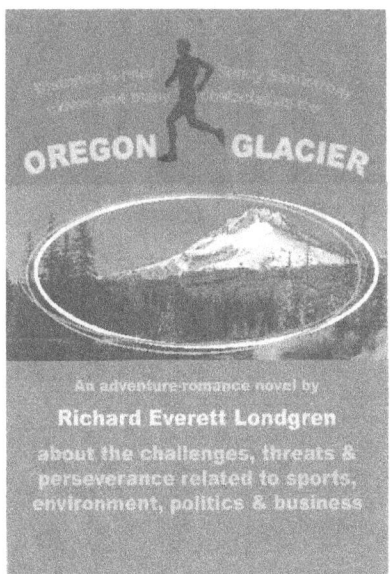

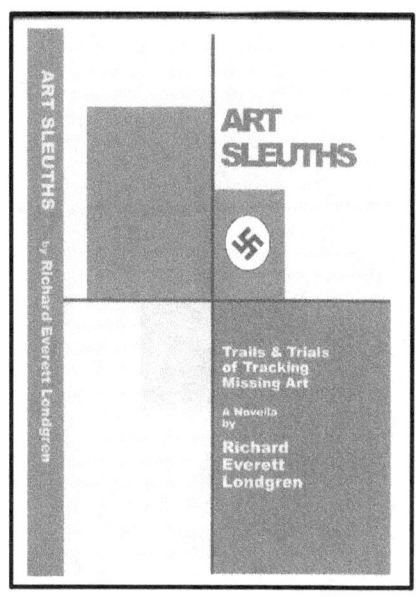

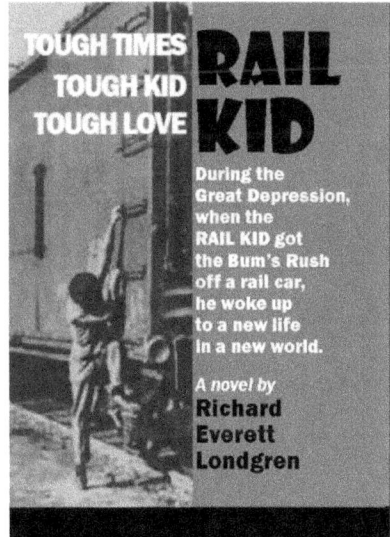

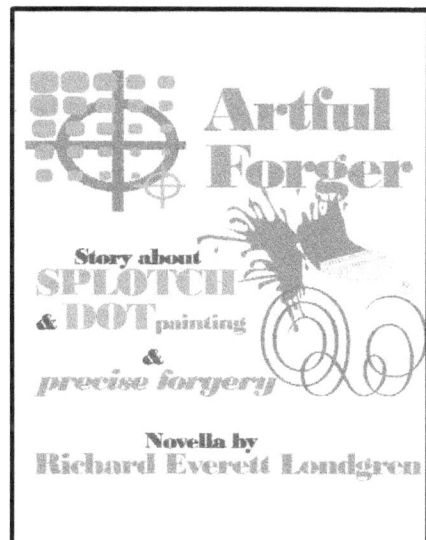

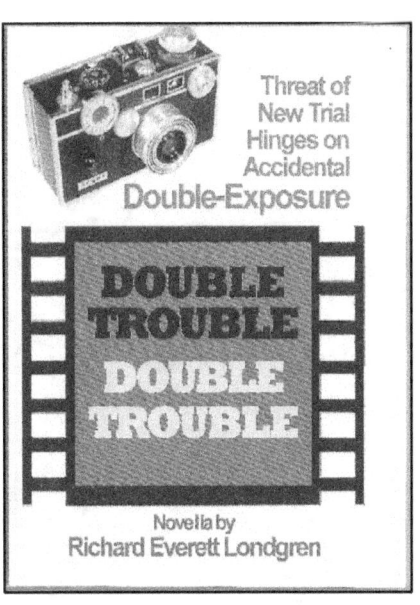

Threat of New Trial Hinges on Accidental Double-Exposure

DOUBLE TROUBLE DOUBLE TROUBLE

Novella by Richard Everett Londgren

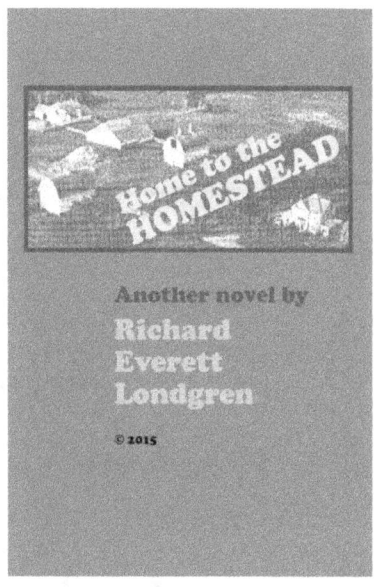

Home to the HOMESTEAD

Another novel by Richard Everett Londgren

© 2015

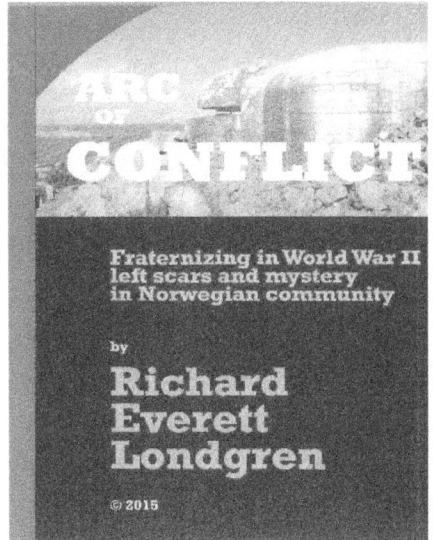

ARC of CONFLICT

Fraternizing in World War II left scars and mystery in Norwegian community

by Richard Everett Londgren

© 2015

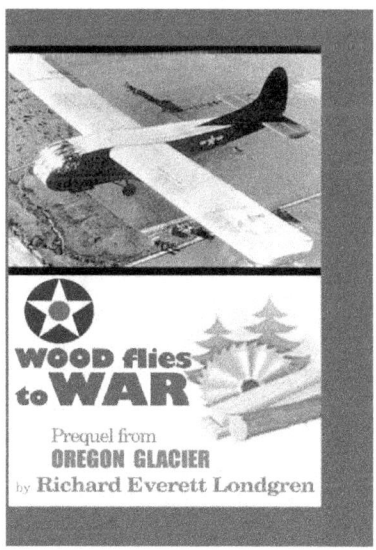

WOOD flies to WAR

Prequel from OREGON GLACIER by Richard Everett Londgren

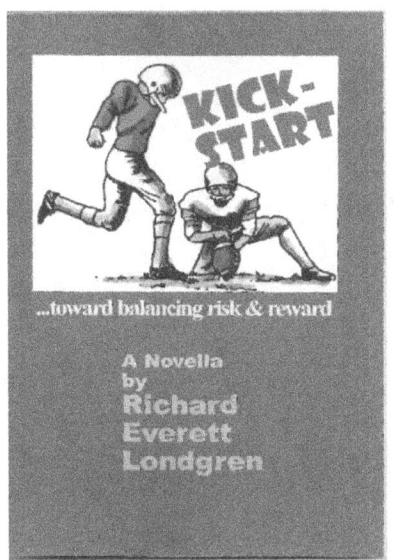

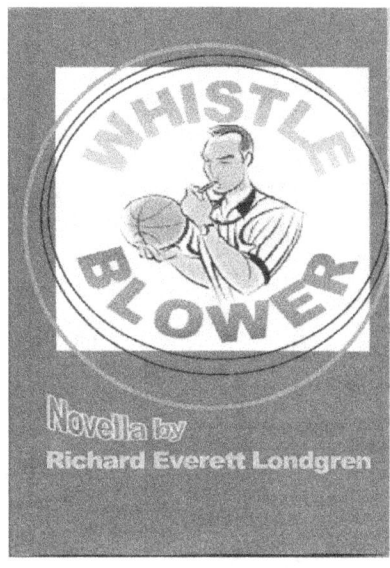

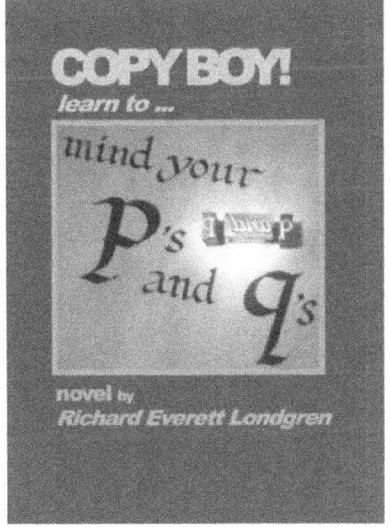

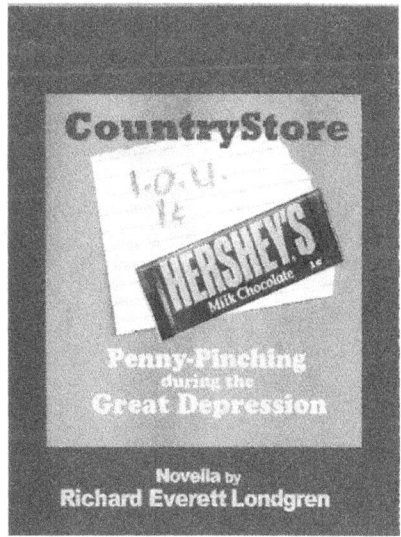

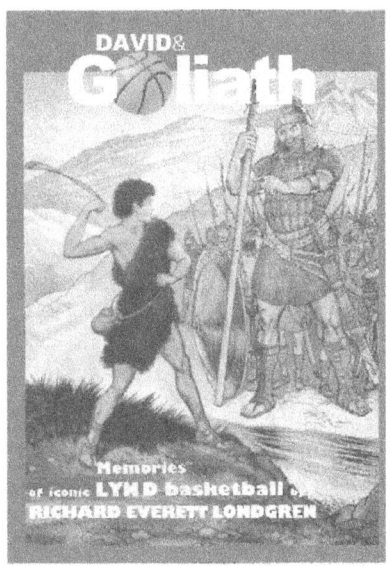

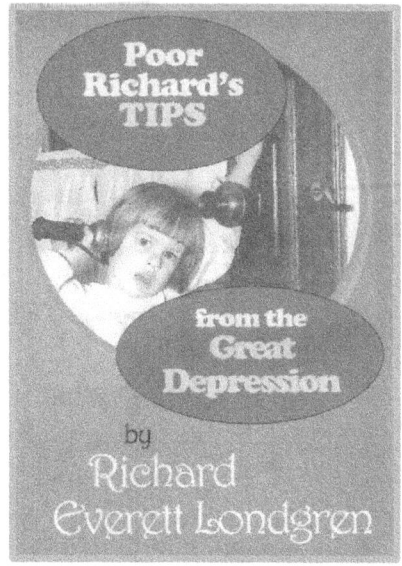

Look for my **Krona** books as shown here—available via Amazon Kindle and print-on-demand paperbacks.

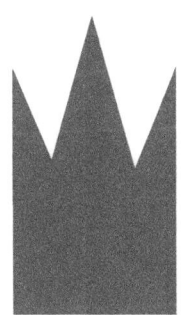

Also check at Barnes & Noble for Nook and print-on-demand paperbacks.

Learn more on my Facebook:

**Richard Londgren Books**